Network Automation with Ansible and NETCONF

James Relington

DEDICATION

To those who seek knowledge, inspiration, and new perspectives—
may this book be a companion on your journey, a spark for curiosity,
and a reminder that every page turned is a step toward discovery.

AKNOWLEDGEMENTS

I would like to express my deepest gratitude to everyone who contributed to the creation of this book. To my colleagues and mentors, your insights and expertise have been invaluable. A special thank you to my family and friends for their unwavering support and encouragement throughout this journey.

Introduction to Network Automation

Network automation is the process of using software to automatically configure, manage, monitor, and operate network devices and services. It leverages tools and technologies that allow network administrators to move away from manual, time-consuming processes toward more efficient, reliable, and scalable workflows. The growth of cloud computing, virtualization, and the increasing complexity of modern networks have made manual configuration and management increasingly unsustainable. Network automation enables organizations to reduce human error, improve consistency, and enhance the agility of their networks. With the widespread adoption of network automation, network administrators can focus on more strategic initiatives, while automation handles repetitive and routine tasks.

One of the primary motivations behind the rise of network automation is the need for faster service delivery. As businesses expand and become more reliant on digital services, their networks must be able to scale quickly and efficiently. Manual configuration methods simply cannot keep pace with the demands of modern infrastructure. Automation solves this problem by allowing network devices to be configured and managed through software-defined processes, reducing the amount of time and effort required to implement changes across multiple devices simultaneously. This is especially critical in environments with large, dynamic networks where agility is essential to keep up with business needs.

Furthermore, network automation improves consistency across the network. Manual configurations are prone to human error, which can lead to misconfigurations, downtime, or security vulnerabilities. By automating the network management process, organizations can ensure that every device is configured according to predefined standards, reducing the risk of inconsistency and mistakes. Automation also enhances compliance by ensuring that network devices are consistently configured to meet security policies and industry regulations. Network administrators can set policies that define how devices should be configured, and the automation tools will enforce these policies, minimizing the chances of non-compliant configurations.

Another significant advantage of network automation is its ability to improve operational efficiency. Automation tools can handle tasks like monitoring, troubleshooting, and performance optimization, allowing network administrators to focus on more critical issues that require human expertise. For example, when network issues arise, automation tools can help quickly identify the root cause and apply fixes, which minimizes downtime and keeps operations running smoothly. This can be especially beneficial in large-scale networks, where manual troubleshooting would be inefficient and time-consuming. Automated systems can also monitor network traffic and performance in real-time, providing network administrators with instant alerts when thresholds are breached or anomalies are detected. This proactive monitoring allows for quicker intervention before problems escalate into major outages.

In addition to improving efficiency, automation also facilitates better collaboration between teams. In traditional network management, different teams—such as the network operations team, security team, and application team—often work in silos. However, network automation fosters a more collaborative environment, where automated processes are standardized and accessible to all teams. This transparency makes it easier to share information, troubleshoot issues collectively, and ensure that all stakeholders are aligned in their efforts. Automation tools can also integrate with other systems, such as configuration management databases (CMDB) and IT service management (ITSM) platforms, to streamline workflows and provide a holistic view of the network environment.

As organizations continue to adopt new technologies such as software-defined networking (SDN) and network function virtualization (NFV), network automation becomes even more essential. These technologies rely heavily on automation to manage network resources dynamically and efficiently. In SDN, for example, network devices are abstracted and controlled by a central software controller, which requires automation to manage configuration changes, policy enforcement, and network topology. Similarly, NFV allows network services to be virtualized and deployed on commodity hardware, which demands automation for the provisioning and management of virtualized network functions (VNFs). Automation thus becomes a key enabler of these modern networking paradigms, allowing organizations to fully realize the benefits of SDN and NFV in terms of flexibility, scalability, and cost savings.

One of the most popular tools used in network automation today is Ansible, a powerful automation platform that enables the orchestration of network tasks. Ansible simplifies the process of automating network configurations and management by using a declarative approach. Rather than specifying step-by-step instructions for every task, network administrators can describe the desired state of a device or service, and Ansible will ensure that the system reaches that state. This declarative model makes it easier to manage complex networks and allows for greater flexibility in handling changes and updates. Additionally, Ansible's simplicity and ease of use make it an appealing choice for network automation, especially in environments where network administrators may not have extensive programming experience.

Another technology that plays a significant role in network automation is NETCONF, a protocol that provides a standardized way to manage network devices. NETCONF uses XML-based messages to interact with network devices and allows for the retrieval and modification of configurations. It is widely used in combination with YANG, a data modeling language that defines the structure of network configurations. NETCONF and YANG work together to provide a robust framework for automating network management tasks, including configuration retrieval, validation, and modification. The combination of NETCONF and Ansible allows for seamless automation of network devices, enabling administrators to configure devices, retrieve configuration data, and enforce policies all through automated workflows.

The adoption of network automation is not without its challenges, however. One of the primary concerns is the complexity of managing automation tools and processes across a diverse network environment. Network devices vary widely in terms of their capabilities, interfaces, and configurations, which can make it difficult to implement a unified automation strategy. Additionally, the learning curve associated with automation tools can be steep, particularly for organizations that are new to automation. Network administrators must also ensure that automation scripts and workflows are tested thoroughly to avoid unintended consequences or errors that could disrupt network operations. Despite these challenges, the benefits of network automation far outweigh the potential risks, and with the right tools and practices in place, organizations can effectively automate their networks to achieve greater efficiency, reliability, and scalability.

In summary, network automation is transforming the way networks are managed and operated. By replacing manual configuration and management tasks with automated processes, organizations can improve efficiency, reduce errors, and enhance the scalability of their networks. The rise of modern technologies like SDN, NFV, and automation platforms like Ansible and NETCONF has made network automation an essential component of modern IT infrastructure. While there are challenges to overcome, the benefits of automation make it a worthwhile investment for organizations looking to streamline their network operations and stay competitive in an increasingly digital world.

Overview of Ansible for Network Automation

Ansible is a powerful and popular automation tool that has gained widespread adoption in network automation. It provides a simple and effective way to automate complex network tasks, such as configuration management, application deployment, and orchestration, with minimal overhead and complexity. Unlike traditional scripting tools that require extensive programming knowledge, Ansible is designed to be user-friendly, relying on a declarative approach to define network states and using easy-to-understand YAML files for configuration. This simplicity, combined with its scalability and flexibility, has made Ansible a go-to solution for network administrators looking to automate tasks across a range of devices and services.

One of the core strengths of Ansible is its agentless architecture. In contrast to other automation tools that require installing agents on managed devices, Ansible operates over SSH or WinRM, which means there is no need to install or maintain additional software on the network devices being managed. This reduces the overhead of managing agents and ensures that network devices are not burdened with unnecessary processes. By using SSH for communication, Ansible simplifies security management, as no special ports or firewall exceptions need to be configured. This agentless nature makes Ansible particularly well-suited for network automation, where devices can range from routers and switches to firewalls and load balancers.

Ansible's declarative model for automation is another key feature that differentiates it from other tools. In a declarative system, the user specifies the desired state of a network device or configuration, rather than outlining the specific steps needed to achieve that state. This approach allows for greater flexibility and reduces the complexity of automation tasks. The user simply defines the desired outcome, such as configuring an interface on a router or deploying a firewall rule, and Ansible ensures that the device is configured accordingly. This declarative method also allows for easier management of large-scale network environments, where keeping track of manual steps can be cumbersome and error-prone. Once a network device is in the desired state, Ansible ensures it remains there, making the process of network management more predictable and reliable.

Ansible's simplicity is reflected in its playbooks, which are written in YAML (YAML Ain't Markup Language). YAML is a human-readable data serialization format that allows users to define complex automation workflows in a straightforward and concise manner. Playbooks are the heart of Ansible automation, containing a series of tasks that are executed on managed devices. Each task describes an action to be taken, such as configuring a device or retrieving information from it. Playbooks can be easily written, shared, and maintained, making them ideal for automating repetitive tasks across a variety of network devices. The simplicity of YAML also means that users do not need to have deep programming knowledge to work with Ansible, further lowering the barrier to entry for network automation.

The use of roles in Ansible allows for better organization and reuse of automation code. Roles enable users to group tasks, variables, files, and templates that are related to a specific function or device type into a self-contained unit. This modular approach allows for greater reusability and flexibility in automation workflows, as roles can be shared and reused across different projects or network environments. For example, a role for configuring a Cisco router can be created and reused for multiple devices, ensuring consistency across the network. Roles also facilitate collaboration between teams, as different team members can work on different roles without interfering with each other's work. This modular approach is particularly useful in large-scale environments where automation tasks need to be organized and managed effectively.

Another key feature of Ansible is its extensibility. Ansible provides a wide range of built-in modules that support various network devices and vendors, such as Cisco, Juniper, Arista, and others. These modules enable users to automate tasks specific to different types of devices, including configuration management, firmware upgrades, and troubleshooting. However, Ansible also allows users to develop their own custom modules if the built-in modules do not meet their needs. Custom modules can be written in any language, although Python is commonly used due to its simplicity and power. This extensibility ensures that Ansible can be used to automate almost any network task, regardless of the device or vendor, making it a versatile solution for modern network environments.

Ansible's ability to integrate with other network management tools is another reason it is well-suited for network automation. Ansible can interact with systems like SNMP, NETCONF, and REST APIs to collect information, make configuration changes, and monitor network devices. For example, Ansible can be used to automate the retrieval of configuration data from a router using NETCONF, or to integrate with monitoring systems to check the health of devices. By combining Ansible's automation capabilities with other tools, network administrators can build a comprehensive automation platform that addresses all aspects of network management, from provisioning and configuration to monitoring and troubleshooting.

One of the significant benefits of using Ansible for network automation is the speed at which changes can be implemented across a network. Whether configuring a single device or thousands, Ansible allows for the rapid execution of tasks. This is particularly valuable in environments where networks are large and dynamic, and quick changes are necessary to maintain operational efficiency. The ability to automate tasks like device provisioning, configuration, and updates means that network administrators can reduce the time spent on routine maintenance and focus on more strategic initiatives. Additionally, Ansible's parallel execution model allows tasks to be executed across multiple devices simultaneously, further speeding up the automation process.

Security is a critical consideration in any network automation workflow, and Ansible addresses this concern by providing several built-in security features. Ansible can use secure connections over SSH or WinRM to communicate with devices, ensuring that data transmitted between the management system and network devices is encrypted. Ansible also supports role-based access control (RBAC), which allows administrators to define which users or groups have permission to execute specific tasks. This ensures that only authorized personnel can make changes to network devices, reducing the risk of unauthorized access or accidental misconfigurations.

Ansible is also well-suited for continuous integration and continuous deployment (CI/CD) workflows. As networks become more dynamic, changes need to be tested and deployed quickly to ensure that they do not disrupt service. Ansible can be integrated with CI/CD tools like Jenkins, GitLab, and others, allowing for the automated testing and deployment of network configurations. This integration ensures that any changes made to the network are tested thoroughly before being applied, reducing the risk of errors and downtime.

Ansible's popularity in network automation is a testament to its effectiveness and ease of use. By providing a simple, declarative approach to network management, Ansible allows network administrators to automate complex tasks with minimal effort. Its agentless architecture, extensibility, and integration capabilities make it an ideal choice for automating a wide range of network tasks. As networks continue to grow in complexity, Ansible will remain a crucial tool for simplifying network management and improving operational efficiency. With its flexibility and scalability, Ansible is well-positioned to meet the evolving needs of modern network environments.

Introduction to NETCONF and YANG

NETCONF (Network Configuration Protocol) and YANG (Yet Another Next Generation) are key technologies that have transformed how network configurations are managed and automated. As networks become increasingly complex and dynamic, traditional methods of configuration management, which rely heavily on manual processes and proprietary protocols, are no longer sufficient to meet the demands of modern network environments. NETCONF and YANG address this challenge by providing standardized mechanisms for configuring, managing, and monitoring network devices in a flexible and scalable manner. These technologies enable automation, integration, and the ability to manage multi-vendor network environments efficiently. NETCONF and YANG together form a powerful combination that enhances network management capabilities, particularly in environments where agility, consistency, and automation are paramount.

NETCONF is a network management protocol defined by the IETF (Internet Engineering Task Force) that provides a standardized way to manage network devices. It is designed to facilitate communication between network management systems and network devices, allowing for the configuration, retrieval, and modification of device configurations in a structured and predictable manner. Unlike traditional configuration methods, which often rely on command-line interfaces (CLI) or simple text-based protocols like SNMP, NETCONF uses XML-based messages to interact with network devices. This approach allows for more granular control over network configurations and ensures that changes are applied consistently and reliably. NETCONF is designed to be extensible, meaning that it can be adapted to different types of network devices, from routers and switches to firewalls and load balancers.

One of the primary advantages of NETCONF is its ability to perform transactional operations. This means that configuration changes made to a network device are not applied until they have been fully validated and approved. In traditional CLI-based management, configuration changes are often applied immediately, and there is no inherent mechanism to roll back changes if something goes wrong. With NETCONF, changes are made in a staged manner, where the configuration is first validated and only committed if it passes all checks. This transactional model helps reduce the risk of misconfigurations and ensures that network devices are always in a known, stable state. If an error occurs, NETCONF allows administrators to roll back to the previous configuration, ensuring minimal disruption to network services.

YANG, on the other hand, is a data modeling language used in conjunction with NETCONF to define the structure of network configurations. While NETCONF handles the communication and operation of network devices, YANG defines the format and structure of the data being communicated. YANG models represent the configuration and operational state of network devices in a standardized and machine-readable format. These models are crucial for ensuring that configuration data is consistent and interoperable across different devices and vendors. YANG allows network administrators to define exactly what data should be included in a device's configuration, what data can be retrieved from the device, and how the data should be formatted. This standardization simplifies the management of multi-vendor environments, where devices from different manufacturers must be configured and monitored using a consistent approach.

The relationship between NETCONF and YANG is symbiotic. NETCONF relies on YANG models to define how configuration data should be structured and validated. When a network administrator issues a command to configure a device via NETCONF, the data is described using a YANG model, ensuring that the data is correctly formatted and adheres to the standards set by the network vendor. This tight integration between NETCONF and YANG allows for a more consistent and streamlined approach to network automation and management. By leveraging YANG's structured data models, NETCONF can handle a wide range of devices and configurations, even in complex multi-vendor environments. This makes NETCONF and YANG an ideal solution for organizations that need to manage diverse networks with a high degree of flexibility and interoperability.

In addition to providing a standardized framework for configuration management, NETCONF and YANG enable automation and orchestration. Automation is one of the primary drivers behind the adoption of NETCONF and YANG in modern network environments. By using NETCONF, network administrators can automate routine tasks such as configuring devices, retrieving device information, and applying updates or patches. These tasks, which would traditionally require manual intervention, can now be performed automatically and consistently across multiple devices, significantly reducing the time and effort required for network management. The use of YANG models in automation scripts ensures that configuration data is structured correctly, minimizing the risk of errors and inconsistencies.

NETCONF and YANG also support the concept of model-driven management. In a model-driven approach, network devices are managed based on predefined data models, rather than being configured using vendor-specific CLI commands or proprietary protocols. This model-driven approach simplifies the management of network devices by abstracting away the details of the underlying hardware and software. Network administrators can work with standardized models that describe the desired state of a network device, regardless of the specific vendor or device type. This makes it easier to manage large, heterogeneous networks with a mix of devices from different vendors, as the same configuration models can be applied across all devices, regardless of their specific implementation.

Another important feature of NETCONF and YANG is their support for real-time monitoring and diagnostics. While NETCONF is primarily focused on configuration management, it also provides capabilities for monitoring the operational state of network devices. By using NETCONF, network administrators can retrieve real-time performance data, such as interface statistics, routing information, and system health metrics. This enables proactive monitoring of network devices, allowing administrators to identify issues before they impact network performance. YANG models can also be used to define the data that should be collected for monitoring purposes, ensuring that the right metrics are captured in a consistent and standardized manner.

The ability to integrate NETCONF and YANG with other network management tools further enhances their value. For example, NETCONF can be integrated with network orchestration platforms, configuration management systems, and monitoring tools to create a comprehensive network management solution. By using NETCONF and YANG in combination with other automation platforms like Ansible, network administrators can automate end-to-end workflows, from device provisioning to configuration management and monitoring. This integration allows for a more holistic approach to network automation, reducing the complexity of managing networks and improving overall operational efficiency.

One of the challenges associated with implementing NETCONF and YANG is the need for network vendors to adopt and support these standards. While many leading networking vendors have embraced NETCONF and YANG, there are still some vendors that rely on proprietary management protocols. However, as the demand for standardized network management continues to grow, more vendors are expected to adopt NETCONF and YANG, ensuring greater interoperability and flexibility in multi-vendor environments. Additionally, the open-source community has played a significant role in driving the adoption of NETCONF and YANG, with numerous tools and libraries available to facilitate the implementation of these technologies.

NETCONF and YANG represent a significant shift in how network devices are managed, moving away from traditional, manual configuration methods toward a more standardized, automated, and scalable approach. By providing a clear structure for managing network configurations and enabling automation, these technologies help organizations reduce the complexity and risk associated with network management. As the networking landscape continues to evolve, NETCONF and YANG will remain central to the management of modern, dynamic networks, enabling organizations to achieve greater efficiency, flexibility, and control over their network infrastructures.

Understanding Declarative Configuration

Declarative configuration is a fundamental concept in modern network management and automation that contrasts sharply with imperative configuration methods. In an imperative configuration model, network administrators must define the specific sequence of steps to achieve a desired state, focusing on the "how" of the configuration process. This approach often requires intricate, manual intervention, and the configuration process can become complex, especially as networks scale and become more dynamic. Declarative configuration, on the other hand, simplifies this process by focusing on the "what" — that is, specifying the desired state of the system rather than the individual steps needed to achieve that state. This approach provides a higher-level abstraction that allows administrators to define the outcome they want without worrying about the underlying details of how the system reaches that point.

The key advantage of declarative configuration is its ability to abstract away the complexities of manual configuration tasks. Network administrators can simply describe the desired state of their network, and the automation tool or system takes care of the implementation details. For example, rather than manually configuring each network device to ensure it meets a particular policy or setting, administrators can define the desired outcome using a declarative configuration

19

model, and the system automatically applies the necessary changes across all relevant devices. This results in significant time savings, as well as a more consistent and predictable configuration process. Declarative configuration helps reduce human error, a common problem in manual configuration approaches, as it ensures that the desired state is applied uniformly across the network.

Another key benefit of declarative configuration is its inherent support for idempotency. In a declarative model, the system checks the current state of the network and compares it to the desired state specified by the administrator. If the current state already matches the desired state, no changes are made. This prevents unnecessary reconfiguration and ensures that the network is not disrupted by repeated configuration changes. Idempotency is especially important in large-scale networks where making unnecessary changes could result in downtime or performance degradation. By using declarative configuration, network administrators can ensure that their networks are configured in a consistent and stable manner, without the risk of unintentionally introducing errors or disruptions.

Declarative configuration is particularly well-suited for network automation, as it aligns perfectly with the principles of automation tools like Ansible, NETCONF, and others. In traditional network management, administrators often had to create scripts or manually enter commands to configure devices. These scripts were typically imperative, specifying the exact sequence of steps to take. However, automation tools that use a declarative model, such as Ansible, allow administrators to define the desired end state in simple, human-readable formats like YAML. The system then handles the execution, ensuring that the network reaches the specified state, regardless of the current configuration of the devices. This declarative approach simplifies the complexity of managing large networks and enables more efficient and scalable automation workflows.

The use of declarative configuration models extends beyond simple network settings to more complex network functions. In large-scale environments, network configurations can often span multiple devices and involve intricate dependencies. With imperative configuration methods, managing these dependencies manually can become cumbersome and error-prone. Declarative configuration, however, allows administrators to define the desired state of the entire network, including the relationships and dependencies between devices and configurations. This makes it easier to manage complex configurations that span multiple devices, reducing the likelihood of misconfigurations or inconsistencies between different parts of the network.

One of the core features of declarative configuration is its ability to ensure consistency across the network. By focusing on the desired state rather than the process of achieving that state, administrators can ensure that all devices are configured according to a uniform set of policies and guidelines. This is particularly important in multi-vendor environments, where different devices from different manufacturers may have different configuration mechanisms and capabilities. A declarative model provides a way to abstract these differences, allowing administrators to define consistent network policies that can be applied across various devices, regardless of their manufacturer or model. This consistency is essential for large-scale networks, where managing configuration drift — the tendency for network devices to diverge from a common configuration over time — can be a significant challenge.

Declarative configuration also plays a crucial role in network troubleshooting and maintenance. In traditional network management, diagnosing configuration issues often involves reviewing complex, imperative scripts or manually checking the configuration of each individual device. With declarative configuration, however, troubleshooting becomes simpler because administrators can compare the current state of the network to the desired state. If a discrepancy is found, it is immediately apparent which devices or settings are out of sync with the desired configuration. This makes it easier to identify and resolve configuration issues quickly, reducing the amount of time spent on manual troubleshooting and minimizing the risk of network outages or performance issues.

As networks continue to grow and evolve, the need for scalable and flexible configuration management solutions becomes more pressing. Declarative configuration addresses this challenge by providing a framework that can scale with the needs of modern networks. Whether managing a small network with just a few devices or a large, global infrastructure with thousands of devices, declarative configuration allows administrators to define and maintain the desired state of the entire network in a manageable and efficient way. This scalability is critical in today's fast-paced and rapidly changing network environments, where the demands for speed, flexibility, and reliability are constantly increasing.

Another key aspect of declarative configuration is its ability to support version control and change management. In traditional network management, keeping track of configuration changes can be difficult, especially when changes are made manually or through complex scripts. Declarative configuration models, however, provide a clear record of the desired state, making it easier to track changes and manage versions. Administrators can store the desired configuration in version-controlled files, such as Git repositories, and easily roll back to previous versions if necessary. This not only helps maintain a history of network configurations but also enables more robust change management practices, ensuring that network changes are applied in a controlled and auditable manner.

The rise of cloud computing and software-defined networking (SDN) has further accelerated the adoption of declarative configuration models. Cloud environments often involve dynamic and rapidly changing network configurations, which makes manual configuration management increasingly impractical. In SDN, the network is abstracted and controlled through software, and declarative configuration is an ideal approach for managing these software-driven networks. By using declarative models, network administrators can define the desired state of the network, and SDN controllers can automatically apply the necessary configurations, making the network more agile, responsive, and adaptable to changing conditions.

In conclusion, declarative configuration offers a powerful and efficient way to manage network configurations in modern, dynamic environments. By focusing on the desired state of the network rather than the specific steps to achieve it, declarative configuration simplifies the process of network management, reduces the risk of human error, and enhances consistency and scalability. Whether used in conjunction with network automation tools like Ansible or as part of software-defined networking frameworks, declarative configuration provides a flexible and robust approach to managing network devices and services. As networks continue to grow in complexity, the adoption of declarative configuration models will be essential for maintaining efficient, reliable, and consistent network operations.

Benefits of Automating Network Configurations

Automating network configurations has become an essential practice for organizations aiming to enhance the efficiency, reliability, and scalability of their networks. As networks grow in size and complexity, manual configuration methods quickly become impractical and error-prone. The need to manage an ever-expanding number of devices, services, and policies calls for a more systematic and automated approach to network management. Network automation offers numerous benefits, including reducing human error, improving consistency, accelerating deployment times, and enabling better scalability. By automating network configurations, organizations can achieve a higher level of control over their infrastructure, while also improving operational efficiency and reducing the risk of network outages or security vulnerabilities.

One of the most significant advantages of automating network configurations is the reduction of human error. Network administrators often have to manually configure devices, enter commands, and ensure that settings are applied correctly. In large-scale networks, even small mistakes can lead to significant issues, such as misconfigurations, service disruptions, or security vulnerabilities. By automating network configurations, organizations minimize the reliance on human intervention and reduce the likelihood of errors. Automation tools ensure that configurations are applied consistently and accurately across all devices, helping to eliminate inconsistencies that might arise from manual processes. This, in turn, enhances network stability and reliability, as administrators can trust that configurations are deployed in the intended manner without the risk of accidental mistakes.

Consistency is another key benefit of automating network configurations. In traditional, manual network management, it is easy for configurations to drift over time, as devices may be configured differently or updated inconsistently. This is particularly true in large networks with multiple devices from different vendors. Manual configuration processes often lack standardization, which can lead to inconsistent settings and varying device behaviors. By automating network configurations, administrators can enforce uniformity across all devices, ensuring that they adhere to the same configuration policies and settings. Automation allows for the application of predefined templates or configurations, ensuring that all network devices are configured consistently. This consistency simplifies troubleshooting, as administrators can be confident that all devices are operating under the same set of rules and settings.

The speed of deployment is significantly improved through automation, particularly in large-scale environments. Manual configuration of devices, especially when deploying changes across hundreds or thousands of devices, is time-consuming and labor-intensive. Automation, on the other hand, enables configurations to be applied quickly and simultaneously across multiple devices, reducing the time required for tasks such as device provisioning, software updates, or policy enforcement. This speed not only accelerates the time to market for new services but also improves network agility, allowing organizations to respond faster to changing business requirements or technological advancements. In dynamic network environments, where devices are constantly being added, removed, or modified, the ability to rapidly deploy configurations ensures that the network can evolve with minimal disruption to ongoing operations.

Automation also enhances scalability, making it easier to manage larger and more complex networks. As businesses expand and networks grow, manually managing configurations becomes increasingly difficult. Automation tools can handle the increased workload, allowing network administrators to scale their configurations across a larger number of devices without being overwhelmed. Automation enables the creation of repeatable processes and templates that can be applied to a growing number of devices as needed. This scalability is crucial for modern enterprises, where networks are frequently expanded to accommodate new offices, data centers, or cloud-based resources. With automation, administrators can ensure that network configurations remain consistent and compliant as the network scales, without sacrificing quality or performance.

In addition to improving operational efficiency, automating network configurations can also help organizations enhance security. Security is a critical concern in modern network environments, where cyberattacks and data breaches are increasingly common. Manual configuration processes often introduce gaps in security, as administrators may overlook or misconfigure certain security settings. Automation can help mitigate these risks by ensuring that security policies are consistently applied across all devices and that the latest security updates are deployed promptly. Automated systems can also be configured to check for compliance with security best practices, such as ensuring that firewalls are properly configured, encryption is enabled, and access controls are in place. By automating security configurations, organizations can reduce the risk of vulnerabilities and enhance their overall security posture.

Another benefit of network configuration automation is the ability to improve troubleshooting and diagnostics. In a traditional, manual configuration environment, diagnosing network issues can be a time-consuming process. Administrators may have to manually inspect configurations, check logs, and make changes to devices one at a time. With automation, however, troubleshooting becomes more efficient. Automation tools can be used to collect and analyze configuration data across multiple devices, enabling administrators to quickly identify discrepancies or issues. If a network problem arises, automation can also help apply fixes or updates across the network without requiring manual intervention. This proactive approach to troubleshooting ensures that issues are addressed quickly and minimizes downtime, ultimately improving the overall performance and reliability of the network.

Network configuration automation also allows organizations to better manage network compliance. Many industries are subject to regulatory requirements that dictate how network devices should be configured, monitored, and maintained. Manual configuration processes can be prone to non-compliance, as administrators may inadvertently overlook or misinterpret regulatory requirements. Automation tools, however, can ensure that network devices are consistently configured according to regulatory standards. Compliance checks can be integrated into automation workflows, allowing administrators to verify that devices are configured correctly and remain compliant with industry regulations. This reduces the risk of non-compliance penalties and ensures that the organization's network infrastructure meets all relevant standards.

Cost efficiency is another compelling reason for automating network configurations. While the initial investment in automation tools may seem high, the long-term savings are substantial. By reducing the need for manual intervention, automation helps organizations cut labor costs associated with network management. Furthermore, automation reduces the risk of costly errors, such as misconfigurations that can lead to network downtime, security breaches, or data loss. The speed and efficiency gains from automation also result in cost savings, as tasks that would traditionally take hours or days to complete can be executed in minutes. Over time, these savings can significantly outweigh the initial investment in automation technologies.

The ability to integrate network automation with other IT and business systems is another benefit that cannot be overlooked. Network automation is not an isolated process; it can be integrated with other tools and platforms, such as configuration management systems, monitoring tools, and ticketing systems. This integration allows for a more cohesive IT environment, where network configurations are aligned with broader IT processes, such as application deployment, incident management, and performance monitoring. Automation platforms can communicate with other systems to ensure that network changes are coordinated with other updates or adjustments, improving overall efficiency and reducing the risk of conflicts between systems.

In a rapidly changing digital landscape, where businesses must adapt to new technologies and increased demand for connectivity, automating network configurations provides the flexibility needed to keep pace. Whether it's supporting the transition to cloud environments, enabling software-defined networking (SDN), or simply managing a growing number of devices and services, network automation helps organizations stay ahead of the curve. By automating network configurations, organizations can improve the consistency, reliability, security, and efficiency of their networks, while also reducing the administrative burden on network teams. This transformation is essential for organizations seeking to maintain competitive advantages in an increasingly connected world.

Chapter: Setting Up Ansible for Network Automation

Ansible has become a powerful tool in the world of network automation, offering an easy-to-use framework for automating network devices and services. To begin utilizing Ansible for network automation, one must first understand how to set it up properly to ensure seamless interaction with network devices. The setup process, while straightforward, requires an understanding of key components, such as Ansible itself, the configuration files, and the various modules that will be used to manage the network infrastructure.

The first step in setting up Ansible for network automation is to install the necessary software on a control machine. The control machine is where Ansible will run the playbooks and communicate with network devices. Ansible can be installed on various operating systems, but the most common setup is on a Linux-based system. The installation process can be done using standard package managers like apt or yum, or it can be done via pip, which is Python's package installer. Once Ansible is installed, it is essential to confirm that the installation was successful by checking the version using the command ansible -- version. This verifies that Ansible is correctly installed and ready to be configured for network automation.

Once Ansible is installed, the next crucial step is to configure the inventory file. The inventory file tells Ansible which devices or groups of devices it will manage. The file is typically structured in an INI or YAML format and specifies the IP addresses or hostnames of the network devices to be managed. The inventory file may also contain additional variables specific to each device, such as username, password, or device-specific configuration settings. Organizing devices into groups can also be very helpful, especially when working with large networks, as it allows the user to apply the same configuration or playbook to multiple devices at once. It is important to ensure that the inventory file is correctly set up, as it is the foundation of all automation tasks in Ansible.

Ansible works by executing playbooks, which are YAML files containing a list of tasks to be carried out on the specified devices. Playbooks are at the heart of network automation, as they define the steps needed to configure, monitor, and manage network devices. When creating a playbook for network automation, it is essential to understand the specific modules that Ansible uses to interact with network devices. Ansible has a rich set of network modules, such as ios_config for Cisco IOS devices, junos_config for Juniper devices, and eos_config for Arista switches. These modules allow Ansible to communicate with devices using protocols like SSH or NETCONF and apply configurations, retrieve status information, or perform other management tasks.

The configuration of network devices can be done in a declarative manner, where the desired state of the device is specified, and Ansible ensures that the device reaches that state. This approach differs from traditional scripting, where users must explicitly define the steps to configure the device. With Ansible, the user simply declares the end state, and Ansible takes care of the rest. For instance, if a user wants to ensure that an interface on a router is configured with a specific IP address, they would define the desired state in the playbook, and Ansible would automatically apply the configuration. This approach not only saves time but also reduces the potential for human error.

To enable communication between Ansible and the network devices, the devices must be accessible via SSH or NETCONF. In the case of NETCONF, which is a protocol used for managing network devices in a more structured way, additional configuration may be required on the devices to enable this communication method. NETCONF provides a more robust and extensible framework for automating network device management, allowing Ansible to push configurations, retrieve operational data, and manage network services. However, it is important to note that NETCONF support varies depending on the vendor and the device's firmware version, so checking the compatibility of NETCONF with the devices in the network is crucial before proceeding with automation.

Another important step in the setup process is ensuring that the necessary Python libraries are installed on the control machine. Ansible relies on various Python modules to communicate with devices, including libraries like Paramiko for SSH connections and ncclient for NETCONF communication. These libraries need to be installed beforehand, as they enable Ansible to interact with the network devices seamlessly. For NETCONF specifically, the ncclient library must be installed, and the user should also be familiar with the library's API to troubleshoot any potential issues.

Once the inventory, playbooks, and communication methods are set up, it is time to test the configuration. The best way to test an Ansible setup is by running a simple playbook that interacts with a network device. For example, a user might write a playbook to retrieve the configuration of a network device and output it to a file. Running this playbook verifies that Ansible can communicate with the device and execute tasks correctly. If any issues arise, Ansible's debugging tools can help identify the problem, such as misconfigured inventory files, missing dependencies, or incorrect device credentials.

As the network automation setup grows, it is important to implement proper security measures to protect sensitive information like device credentials. Ansible provides options like Ansible Vault to encrypt sensitive data within playbooks and inventory files. This ensures that passwords and other sensitive information are stored securely and not exposed in plain text. Vault can also be used to encrypt entire playbooks, providing an extra layer of protection for automated tasks that involve confidential data.

Finally, maintaining an efficient workflow and automation pipeline is key to successful network automation. As the network infrastructure evolves, new devices are added, and configurations change. Ansible's flexibility allows users to quickly adapt to these changes, whether it's by adding new devices to the inventory, updating playbooks to reflect new configuration requirements, or implementing changes to the existing automation setup. Automation with Ansible ensures that the network remains consistent, reliable, and easily manageable, even as it grows in complexity.

Setting up Ansible for network automation is a crucial step in streamlining the management of network devices and services. By understanding how to install, configure, and utilize Ansible effectively, network engineers can significantly reduce manual configuration errors, increase operational efficiency, and achieve a more robust and reliable network infrastructure. With Ansible, network automation becomes not only a possibility but a reality, providing an effective tool for modern network management.

Chapter: Configuring NETCONF Servers

NETCONF, or Network Configuration Protocol, has become an essential tool in the world of network automation. It allows for structured and automated configuration of network devices, providing a robust way to manage networks efficiently. In order to fully leverage NETCONF for network management, one must understand how to configure NETCONF servers properly. This configuration involves enabling NETCONF on the devices themselves, setting up the necessary communication protocols, and ensuring that proper security measures are in place. Each of these steps requires careful attention to ensure that the devices and their network configurations can be managed effectively using NETCONF.

The first step in configuring a NETCONF server is to verify that the network device supports NETCONF. While many modern network devices from vendors like Cisco, Juniper, and Arista support NETCONF, older models may not have this capability. It is important to consult the device documentation to determine whether NETCONF is available and if any specific software or firmware updates are required to enable it. Once it has been confirmed that the device supports NETCONF, the next step is to enable the NETCONF service on the device. This typically involves configuring the device to listen for NETCONF requests and enabling the necessary ports and protocols.

On many devices, enabling NETCONF involves accessing the device's configuration mode and issuing specific commands. For example, in Cisco devices running IOS XE, the command to enable NETCONF is usually entered in global configuration mode with the command netconf-yang. This command ensures that the device is ready to accept NETCONF connections from clients. On Juniper devices, the NETCONF service is enabled through the command set system services netconf ssh, which configures the device to listen for NETCONF over SSH. Once these services are enabled, the device will be able to receive NETCONF requests over the network.

Along with enabling the NETCONF service on the device, it is also necessary to configure the appropriate transport protocols. NETCONF relies heavily on transport protocols like SSH (Secure Shell) to communicate between the server and client. Ensuring that SSH is properly configured on the network device is critical to the success of the NETCONF connection. This involves verifying that the SSH service is running and that proper authentication methods are configured. This may include configuring RSA or ECDSA keys for secure communication and ensuring that user authentication, such as using username and password or public key authentication, is set up correctly.

Once the NETCONF server is enabled and the transport protocols are configured, the next step is to establish user permissions. This is crucial in ensuring that only authorized users have access to the NETCONF server and can make changes to the network device. On many devices, this can be done by configuring user accounts and specifying which users have the necessary privileges to interact with the NETCONF server. For example, in Cisco IOS XE, user roles and permissions are defined using the command username <username> privilege <level>, where the privilege level dictates the user's ability to execute various commands.

Security is one of the most important considerations when configuring a NETCONF server. Since NETCONF allows for the configuration of network devices, it inherently carries some risks. One of the most effective ways to secure NETCONF servers is by using encryption. As NETCONF relies on SSH for transport, the traffic is already encrypted during transit. However, it is important to ensure that strong encryption algorithms are used and that any known vulnerabilities in the SSH service are patched. In addition to encryption, authentication methods should be carefully configured to ensure that only authorized users can access the NETCONF server. This may involve using multi-factor authentication or configuring access control lists (ACLs) to restrict which devices or networks can establish a NETCONF session.

Another key security measure is the use of NETCONF access control lists (ACLs) or role-based access control (RBAC) to control what operations a user can perform on the device. For example, an administrator may configure the NETCONF server so that certain users can only retrieve configuration data or read-only information from the device, while others are allowed to make configuration changes. This level of granularity helps protect the device from unauthorized or unintentional changes, improving the overall security of the network.

For advanced use cases, NETCONF can also be configured to support the YANG data model. YANG is a data modeling language used to define the structure of configuration data and operational data on network devices. By integrating YANG with NETCONF, users can benefit from a more flexible and standardized approach to network automation. YANG models provide a clear definition of the configuration parameters that can be manipulated on a device, making it easier to automate tasks and ensure consistency across the network. Many network vendors now support YANG models, and these models can be loaded onto the device as part of the NETCONF configuration process. This ensures that the device can be configured and managed in a standardized way, using a common schema across different platforms and vendors.

Once the NETCONF server is properly configured, it is time to test the connection. This can be done by using NETCONF clients, such as ncclient, which is a Python library for interacting with NETCONF servers. The client can be used to send requests to the NETCONF server, retrieve configuration data, or apply new configurations. Testing the connection ensures that the server is listening correctly for incoming NETCONF requests and that the appropriate responses are returned. This step is important to confirm that all configurations were done correctly and that communication between the NETCONF server and client is functioning as expected.

Monitoring the NETCONF server after it is set up is also essential to ensure its continued functionality. This involves periodically checking the status of the NETCONF service, reviewing system logs for errors or warnings, and verifying that the device remains accessible via NETCONF. If any issues are detected, troubleshooting tools and commands can be used to identify and resolve the problem. For example, reviewing the SSH configuration or inspecting the transport layer can help address connectivity issues, while examining user permissions can resolve access-related problems.

Configuring a NETCONF server is a critical step in enabling network automation and management. By ensuring that the device is properly configured to support NETCONF, using secure communication methods like SSH, and implementing appropriate security measures, network engineers can create a reliable and secure platform for managing network devices. The integration of YANG models further enhances the flexibility and standardization of the network automation process, making it easier to manage diverse devices from different vendors. Proper testing and ongoing monitoring are necessary to maintain the integrity of the configuration and ensure that the NETCONF server continues to operate effectively. Through careful configuration and management, NETCONF servers provide a powerful tool for network automation, offering an efficient and secure method for handling network device configurations and operational data.

Chapter: Working with Ansible Modules for Network Devices

Ansible has revolutionized the way network configurations and automations are carried out, offering a powerful and flexible framework for managing a variety of network devices. One of the key components that make Ansible so efficient for network automation is its extensive library of modules. These modules are designed to interact with different types of network devices, allowing users to perform tasks such as configuring routers, switches, firewalls, and other devices with minimal effort. Working with these modules requires a basic understanding of how they function, how to integrate them into playbooks, and how to troubleshoot and optimize their use to ensure a smooth automation process.

The Ansible modules for network devices are essentially pre-built scripts that enable automation of tasks on various types of network hardware. These modules abstract the complexity of communicating with network devices by providing a simple and consistent interface for configuring or managing devices, regardless of the vendor. Each module is specific to a particular type of device or protocol, and they support a range of functionalities, from applying configurations to querying device statuses or retrieving logs. For instance, Cisco devices use modules like ios_config, ios_facts, and ios_interface, which allow users to modify configurations, retrieve system facts, and manage interfaces, respectively.

One of the most important aspects of working with Ansible modules for network devices is understanding how to structure playbooks. A playbook is a YAML file that contains one or more plays, and each play describes a set of tasks to be performed on one or more target devices. The playbook will specify which module to use, what parameters to pass to the module, and which devices the playbook will target. For example, a playbook might use the ios_config module to configure an interface on a Cisco router by specifying parameters such as the interface name, IP address, and subnet mask. This abstraction helps network engineers automate repetitive tasks without needing to manually log into each device and apply configurations step by step.

When working with network devices, it is important to understand that Ansible modules communicate with devices using different protocols. Common protocols include SSH, NETCONF, and HTTPS, depending on the device and module being used. Ansible's default method of communication is over SSH, which is widely supported by most network devices. However, some devices, particularly those from vendors like Juniper or Arista, may require NETCONF or other protocols to manage the devices more efficiently. It is crucial to ensure that the network devices are properly configured to support the protocol that the relevant Ansible module requires. This can involve enabling the appropriate services on the device, such as SSH or NETCONF, and ensuring that any firewall or access control settings allow communication from the Ansible control machine.

Another key element of working with Ansible modules is defining the inventory. The inventory is a file that specifies the network devices that the playbook will interact with. It can be as simple as listing a few IP addresses or as complex as defining multiple groups of devices, each with specific variables and settings. By organizing devices into groups, network administrators can easily apply configurations to multiple devices simultaneously. For example, one might have a group for core switches, another for access switches, and another for routers. The advantage of this organization is that playbooks can be written to target specific groups of devices and apply settings uniformly across them. This saves time and ensures consistency when configuring a large network.

Once the inventory and playbooks are defined, the next step is to execute the automation tasks. When running Ansible playbooks, users can specify various options to control the execution. For example, the -v option enables verbose output, which helps in debugging if something goes wrong. If an error occurs, the output will typically provide enough information to diagnose the issue. Additionally, Ansible allows users to limit the execution to specific devices using the --limit flag, making it easier to test changes on a subset of devices before applying them network-wide. This makes Ansible highly flexible and reduces the risk of misconfigurations during automation tasks.

As useful as Ansible modules are, it is important to recognize that they are not infallible and that issues can arise during their execution. One common issue when working with network devices is handling device-specific quirks. Even though Ansible provides modules for a wide range of devices, each vendor may implement certain features or configurations differently. This can lead to situations where a playbook works on one device but fails on another, even if the devices are from the same vendor. To resolve these issues, network engineers often need to refer to vendor-specific documentation to understand how to work around these differences. Ansible's modular approach allows users to extend its functionality by writing custom modules if necessary, which can be tailored to accommodate unique network device requirements.

Another common challenge when using Ansible modules is managing device credentials and security. Since network devices often require authentication to perform configuration changes, securely storing and handling credentials is paramount. Ansible provides tools like Ansible Vault, which allows users to encrypt sensitive information, such as passwords, so that they are not stored in plain text within playbooks or inventory files. Vault uses a symmetric encryption method to ensure that only authorized users with the correct password can access the encrypted data. This feature is essential for maintaining the confidentiality of network configurations and credentials while automating tasks.

Furthermore, Ansible modules for network devices also allow users to retrieve operational data, which is useful for monitoring and troubleshooting network infrastructure. For instance, modules like ios_facts or junos_facts can be used to gather system information such as device version, uptime, and interface statistics. This data can then be used to validate the network state or check for anomalies. By incorporating these facts into playbooks, network engineers can automate not only configuration tasks but also monitoring and reporting processes, making the entire network management lifecycle more efficient and automated.

One of the strengths of Ansible modules is their ability to maintain state consistency across devices. Network devices, unlike traditional servers, often require real-time configuration changes that must be carefully applied to avoid service disruptions. Ansible modules ensure that the desired state is reached without affecting the device's operational stability. The declarative nature of Ansible's configuration model means that users specify the end state of the device, and Ansible takes care of making the necessary adjustments. This approach minimizes the chances of errors, ensures configurations are applied correctly, and helps maintain network stability over time.

In addition to these capabilities, Ansible's network modules support more advanced functionalities, such as managing network topologies, configuring VLANs, routing protocols, and other complex network features. As network automation continues to evolve, Ansible modules will remain a critical part of streamlining network management and ensuring that configurations are applied quickly, securely, and consistently across an entire infrastructure. Whether it's for routine configuration changes or large-scale network upgrades, Ansible provides the tools necessary to automate and simplify the process of working with network devices.

Chapter: The Role of Inventory Files in Ansible Automation

In Ansible automation, the inventory file is one of the most critical components, providing a clear and structured way to define which hosts and devices will be managed during the automation process. The inventory file contains a list of machines or network devices along with their respective details, and it serves as the foundation for all Ansible tasks and playbooks. Understanding the role of the inventory file is essential for users who wish to effectively manage network devices, servers, and infrastructure through Ansible. Without the inventory file, Ansible would not know which devices to target, how to reach them, or what configuration settings to apply. Thus, configuring this file correctly is paramount to ensuring that Ansible's automation capabilities can be fully realized.

The inventory file in Ansible is essentially a dynamic map that links Ansible with the target systems. This file contains the names or IP addresses of the machines that will be configured or managed, and it is where users define how Ansible will connect to those devices. It can be structured in various formats, including the traditional INI format or more modern YAML format. Both formats allow users to specify individual hosts, organize those hosts into groups, and define variables that control how tasks are executed on each device or group. These variables can include authentication credentials, network settings, or specific configuration parameters that tailor automation to the needs of each host or group.

One of the primary benefits of the inventory file is its ability to group hosts into categories. Grouping hosts is especially useful in larger environments where numerous devices may require similar configurations or automation tasks. For example, a network environment may include routers, switches, firewalls, and load balancers, all of which might require different playbooks but could still share common configuration steps. By organizing these devices into groups, such as "routers," "switches," or "firewalls," users can create more manageable and efficient playbooks that target entire groups of devices instead of manually specifying each host individually. This not only simplifies the automation process but also enhances the scalability of the automation, allowing it to adapt to growing infrastructures.

In addition to grouping devices, the inventory file can also contain specific variables and parameters that are assigned to individual hosts or groups. These variables might define things like device IP addresses, login credentials, network interfaces, or other device-specific settings. By defining these variables in the inventory file, users can avoid having to hard-code such values directly into playbooks. This not only improves flexibility but also ensures that playbooks can be reused across different environments without modification. For instance, if a user has an inventory file with multiple routers and each router has a unique login, the user can define a variable for each router's login credentials in the inventory file and then refer to those variables in the playbook.

The inventory file also plays a significant role in controlling access to managed systems. By defining which hosts and groups are available, it determines which systems are available for playbooks to target. This can be particularly important in environments where different users or teams may be responsible for different parts of the network. In such cases, an inventory file can be structured to limit which devices are visible or accessible to particular users, ensuring that only authorized personnel can execute tasks on certain systems. This access control mechanism is essential for maintaining security in complex network environments, where different teams or departments may need to manage their own devices but should not have access to other critical systems.

Another important feature of Ansible's inventory files is their ability to manage dynamic inventories. While static inventory files are hardcoded with a list of hosts, dynamic inventory files can pull information from external sources, such as cloud providers, databases, or network management tools, to create an up-to-date inventory automatically. This is particularly useful in cloud environments where the number of instances may fluctuate frequently. With a dynamic inventory, the inventory file is constantly updated to reflect the actual state of the infrastructure, making it possible for Ansible to always target the correct devices, even as they are added or removed. Dynamic inventories enable automation in environments that are highly dynamic, reducing the need for manual updates to the inventory file.

While the inventory file is crucial for targeting devices, it also supports various methods for defining how Ansible should connect to those devices. Each host or group in the inventory can be configured with connection parameters, such as the connection type (SSH, NETCONF, etc.), user credentials, and any necessary connection options like port numbers or timeouts. This means that the inventory file can serve as a central place to define how Ansible connects to different types of devices across the network. For example, if a network device supports NETCONF, the inventory file can specify that the NETCONF protocol should be used for communication, while a server might require SSH for management. This centralized management of connection settings allows for easier troubleshooting and management of large-scale network environments.

Ansible also provides flexibility when it comes to organizing the inventory file. In large, complex networks, the inventory file might become quite large, with many hosts and groups defined. To simplify management, users can split the inventory file into multiple smaller files, which can then be included in a master inventory file. This modular approach makes it easier to manage large inventories, especially in organizations with distributed teams or environments where different departments manage different parts of the infrastructure. By breaking up the inventory into smaller, more manageable chunks, users can easily maintain and update their inventories without worrying about a single, monolithic file.

In addition to the ability to define host variables and groups, Ansible also supports host-specific settings within the inventory file. These settings allow for even more precise control over how playbooks are executed on individual hosts. For example, users can define whether a particular host should be treated differently in a playbook, such as by applying different configuration tasks or overriding default behavior. This feature ensures that even within a single group, there can be nuanced differences in how automation is applied, depending on the specific requirements of each device.

The role of inventory files in Ansible automation cannot be overstated. These files are the cornerstone of Ansible's ability to manage diverse infrastructures, providing a mechanism to define which systems are to be managed, how they should be connected, and what variables should be used during automation tasks. By offering a structured and flexible way to define hosts, groups, and variables, the inventory file enables users to automate tasks efficiently, securely, and consistently across a wide range of devices and environments. Whether managing a handful of devices or a large, distributed network, the inventory file serves as the critical interface between Ansible and the systems it manages, ensuring that automation workflows are both effective and adaptable to changing network conditions.

Chapter: YAML Syntax for Network Automation

YAML, or Yet Another Markup Language, has become the standard data serialization format in many areas of IT automation, including network automation. Its readability, simplicity, and flexibility have made it the preferred choice for defining configurations and automation scripts. In the context of network automation, YAML is used to define playbooks and configuration files that drive tasks such as configuring network devices, monitoring network status, and managing infrastructure at scale. Understanding the syntax of YAML is crucial for anyone working with Ansible or similar tools in network automation, as it directly influences the way automation tasks are written and executed.

The primary strength of YAML lies in its human-readable structure. Unlike other markup languages, YAML emphasizes simplicity, using indentation to represent nested structures rather than complex punctuation. This makes it intuitive for network engineers and IT professionals to work with, as it closely mirrors natural language. A basic YAML structure consists of key-value pairs, where the key represents an attribute, and the value is the associated data. These key-value pairs can be scalars, lists, or dictionaries, allowing YAML to model a wide range of data types.

In network automation, the most common use of YAML is in Ansible playbooks, which define the tasks to be executed on network devices. Each playbook consists of one or more plays, and each play represents a set of tasks that will be applied to one or more hosts. YAML syntax in Ansible is used to specify not only the hosts and tasks but also variables, conditions, and modules. For example, when writing a playbook to configure a Cisco router, the YAML structure would include the tasks to modify interface configurations, apply routing protocols, or update access control lists, all structured within a simple, easy-to-read format.

At the heart of YAML syntax is indentation. Indentation indicates hierarchical relationships between elements. For example, a list of tasks within a play is indented under the task section, and a list of hosts is indented under the hosts section. This indentation is critical, as it dictates the structure and relationships between different parts of the YAML file. Each level of indentation must be consistent, typically using two spaces per indentation level, although some implementations allow four spaces. Incorrect indentation can result in parsing errors, making it important to maintain uniformity throughout the file.

In network automation, it is common to use variables in YAML files to ensure flexibility and reusability of playbooks. Variables are defined by using the syntax key: value, where the key is the name of the variable, and the value is the data assigned to it. These variables can be simple data types like strings, integers, or booleans, or they can be more complex structures like lists or dictionaries. For example, a variable could be used to define the IP address of a router or the username and password needed for SSH access. The ability to use variables allows users to write more general and reusable playbooks, as the same playbook can be executed across multiple devices with different configurations by simply changing the variables.

YAML also supports the use of lists, which are represented by a hyphen followed by a space. Lists are commonly used in network automation when there is a need to define multiple items that share a common attribute. For example, a playbook may include a list of interfaces that need to be configured on a device. In this case, the list would be represented in YAML as a series of lines, each beginning with a hyphen and followed by the interface configuration. Lists can also be used to define multiple tasks, where each task is an item in the list of operations to be executed.

Another powerful feature of YAML is its ability to define dictionaries, which are essentially key-value pairs nested inside other dictionaries or lists. This allows for complex data structures that can represent detailed configurations, such as a device's settings, interface configurations, or access control policies. In network automation, dictionaries are often used to represent device configurations, where the keys are configuration parameters, and the values are the specific settings to be applied. For example, a dictionary might represent the configuration of a network interface, with keys for the interface name, IP address, subnet mask, and description.

YAML also allows the use of comments, which are denoted by the hash symbol (#). Comments are essential for providing explanations or context within a YAML file, especially when dealing with complex configurations. They can be placed on their own line or at the end of a line, following the actual configuration. In network automation, comments are often used to document the purpose of specific tasks or sections of the playbook, making it easier for other users or future maintainers to understand the intent behind the automation.

The flexibility of YAML extends to its support for anchors and aliases, which allow users to reuse parts of the data structure. An anchor is defined by using the & symbol, followed by a name for the anchor. This anchor can then be referenced elsewhere in the file using the alias symbol *. This is particularly useful in network automation when certain configurations or values need to be reused in multiple places within a playbook. By defining an anchor for a commonly used configuration, network engineers can avoid duplicating data and reduce the chance of errors.

Another important aspect of YAML in network automation is the use of conditionals and loops, which provide control over the flow of tasks based on certain criteria. For example, Ansible playbooks often use conditional statements to determine whether a particular task should be executed. These conditions are defined using the when keyword, which allows a task to run only if a specified condition is true. Similarly, loops can be used to repeat a task for a list of items, such as applying a configuration to multiple network interfaces or devices. The combination of conditionals and loops makes YAML a powerful tool for automating complex, repetitive tasks in network environments.

Despite its simplicity, YAML is a powerful tool for network automation due to its flexibility and ease of use. By understanding the basic syntax and structure of YAML, network engineers can leverage it to automate a wide range of tasks, from configuring routers and switches to managing security policies and monitoring network performance. The human-readable nature of YAML allows users to quickly write and understand automation scripts, which is crucial in environments where time and accuracy are of the essence. As network automation continues to grow in importance, YAML will remain a foundational element in making automation accessible and effective.

Chapter: Ansible Playbooks for Networking Tasks

Ansible playbooks are the cornerstone of network automation. Playbooks are written in YAML and are designed to define the tasks that need to be executed on the target systems, whether they are routers, switches, firewalls, or other network devices. In the context of network automation, Ansible playbooks help automate routine network tasks, such as configuring interfaces, managing network protocols, updating device configurations, and deploying new features across an entire infrastructure. Understanding how to write and execute Ansible playbooks is crucial for anyone seeking to streamline network management and reduce manual intervention.

A playbook begins with a structure that defines the hosts or devices the playbook will target. The primary role of a playbook is to group a series of tasks under a set of hosts and then execute those tasks on the targeted devices. This hierarchical approach allows network engineers to manage multiple devices efficiently. By defining specific tasks, users can automate routine configuration changes, apply new security policies, or deploy system updates with minimal human interaction. The tasks themselves are simple and concise, specifying the modules and arguments needed to configure a network device, query its status, or modify its settings.

In the realm of networking, one of the most common tasks in an Ansible playbook is configuring network interfaces. For instance, the ios_config module can be used to configure Cisco devices running IOS, allowing users to apply interface configurations such as IP addresses, subnet masks, and descriptions. The beauty of Ansible playbooks lies in their ability to make these tasks declarative. Instead of manually logging into each device and issuing configuration commands, an engineer can write a playbook that automatically applies the desired configuration to all target devices. This method not only saves time but also reduces the risk of errors that could arise from inconsistent configurations.

Similarly, configuring routing protocols is another common task that can be automated using Ansible playbooks. Networking environments often rely on protocols such as OSPF, BGP, or EIGRP to manage routing decisions across a network. Rather than configuring these protocols manually on each device, an Ansible playbook can be written to automate the process. For example, using the ios_eigrp module, an engineer can quickly configure EIGRP on a Cisco router, applying settings such as the autonomous system number, network statements, and passive interfaces. The playbook would define all the parameters necessary to configure the protocol across multiple routers, ensuring consistency and reducing the need for manual intervention.

Ansible playbooks also excel in managing security configurations on network devices. Whether it is setting up access control lists (ACLs), configuring firewalls, or managing user permissions, Ansible offers modules tailored to each of these tasks. For example, the ios_acl module can be used to automate the creation and application of ACLs on Cisco devices, allowing network engineers to define which traffic should be allowed or denied across network interfaces. These ACLs are vital for controlling network traffic and securing the infrastructure, and automating their deployment ensures that the configurations are consistent and applied across all relevant devices.

In larger environments, where devices are frequently added or removed, managing device configurations can become a tedious task. This is where the power of Ansible's dynamic inventory comes into play. Dynamic inventory allows Ansible to query external sources, such as cloud providers or network management tools, to generate an up-to-date list of devices. This ensures that playbooks are always targeting the correct devices, even as the network topology changes. Dynamic inventory files can be set up to automatically pull information about the network, including the device types, IP addresses, and other critical parameters, allowing the playbook to adapt to a constantly changing network.

Another advantage of using Ansible playbooks is the ability to gather facts from the target devices before applying any changes. Ansible's fact-gathering capabilities allow users to retrieve information about the devices, such as hardware details, interface statuses, system resources, and running configurations. This data can be used to validate the current state of the device and ensure that changes are only applied when certain conditions are met. For example, a playbook might gather facts from a router to check its current routing protocol configuration and then only apply changes if the protocol is not already configured correctly. This dynamic approach helps prevent unnecessary changes and ensures that the network remains in a consistent state.

Managing large-scale network environments often involves working with groups of devices that share similar configurations or roles. Ansible playbooks make it easy to define groups of devices in the inventory file, allowing users to apply configurations to entire groups with a single playbook run. For instance, a user might have a group for core routers, another for edge switches, and another for firewalls. By grouping devices based on their role or location in the network, users can write more efficient playbooks that target specific device categories, applying configurations that are relevant to each group. This grouping mechanism also reduces the complexity of playbooks, as network engineers can target entire clusters of devices without having to individually define each one.

The use of variables in Ansible playbooks further enhances flexibility and reusability. Variables can be defined in the playbook itself, in the inventory file, or in separate files, and they allow users to define device-specific settings such as IP addresses, credentials, or interface names. By using variables, the same playbook can be applied to multiple devices or environments with minimal changes. For example, a playbook that configures a network interface could use a variable for the IP address, enabling it to be reused across different routers or switches with different IP addresses. This approach ensures that the playbook remains adaptable to changing environments and simplifies the process of managing network configurations.

Error handling and task retries are also important features of Ansible playbooks that ensure reliable execution in network automation. In some cases, network devices may be temporarily unreachable, or a task might fail due to a configuration mismatch. Ansible provides options for retrying failed tasks or handling errors gracefully. For example, a playbook might be configured to retry a task up to three times before giving up or to continue with the next task in case of failure. This level of fault tolerance is crucial in production environments, where downtime or misconfigurations can lead to significant disruptions.

As network environments become more complex and dynamic, the role of Ansible playbooks in automating network tasks continues to grow. Playbooks can automate a wide range of tasks, from configuring network interfaces and routing protocols to applying security policies and managing device configurations. By reducing the need for manual configuration, Ansible playbooks help ensure that network infrastructure remains consistent, reliable, and secure. The power of Ansible lies in its ability to automate repetitive tasks, gather device facts, and manage large-scale network environments with ease, providing network engineers with the tools they need to build and maintain complex, high-performance networks.

Chapter: Automating Device Configuration with Ansible

The ability to automate device configuration has become a critical component in modern network management. Ansible, with its simple syntax and powerful automation capabilities, has emerged as a leading tool for streamlining the process of configuring network devices. Traditionally, configuring network devices involved manually logging into each device and entering configuration commands one by one. This method is not only time-consuming but also prone to human error, especially when managing large-scale networks with hundreds or even thousands of devices. Ansible addresses these challenges by allowing network engineers to automate the configuration of network devices through playbooks and modules, reducing the complexity and risk associated with manual configuration.

Ansible's approach to automation is declarative, meaning that network engineers define the desired state of the device rather than the specific steps required to achieve that state. This is a fundamental shift from traditional imperative configuration methods, where the engineer must specify each action in a step-by-step sequence. With Ansible, engineers can simply specify the configuration they want, and Ansible will take care of the necessary steps to ensure the device matches that configuration. For example, a user might define in an Ansible playbook that a router should have an IP address on a particular interface, and Ansible will handle the task of configuring that interface with the correct IP address, subnet mask, and other necessary settings.

The key to automating device configuration with Ansible lies in the use of modules. Ansible provides a vast array of modules specifically designed for interacting with network devices. These modules abstract the complexity of communication protocols like SSH or NETCONF, allowing users to focus on the configuration itself. For instance, the ios_config module is used for configuring Cisco devices running IOS. It allows users to push configuration changes to a device, whether it's configuring interfaces, applying routing protocols, or setting up access control lists. Similarly, there are modules for other devices such as junos_config for Juniper devices and eos_config for Arista switches. These modules provide a standardized interface for interacting with different types of devices, ensuring that playbooks remain portable and reusable across a variety of network infrastructures.

To begin automating device configuration with Ansible, the first step is to define the inventory. The inventory file lists the devices that will be targeted by the playbook and specifies the connection details needed to communicate with them. Devices can be organized into groups, and each group can be assigned specific variables or configuration settings. For example, a group for routers might include variables like the router's IP address, SSH username, and password. Organizing devices into groups is particularly helpful in large networks, as it allows for bulk configuration of similar devices without needing to define each device individually. Once the inventory is set up, Ansible can connect to the devices using SSH or other supported protocols and execute the tasks defined in the playbook.

The next step is writing the playbook itself. A playbook in Ansible is a YAML file that defines a series of tasks to be executed on the target devices. Each task specifies a module to be used, along with the arguments required for that module. For example, if the task is to configure an interface on a Cisco router, the playbook would call the ios_config module and pass it the necessary configuration parameters such as the interface name, IP address, and subnet mask. Ansible's modular design allows users to focus on the specific configuration they wish to apply without worrying about the underlying implementation details of how the module interacts with the device.

One of the most powerful features of Ansible is its ability to ensure that devices reach a desired state, even if they are already partially configured. Ansible playbooks are idempotent, meaning that running the same playbook multiple times on the same device will not result in redundant changes. If the device is already in the desired state, Ansible will skip the task, saving time and resources. This is particularly useful in environments where devices may be reconfigured frequently, or when applying minor changes across a large number of devices. By ensuring that configurations are applied consistently across the network, Ansible helps maintain network stability and reduces the risk of misconfigurations.

In addition to applying configurations, Ansible also allows users to gather information from devices, which can be useful for validation or troubleshooting purposes. Ansible's fact-gathering capabilities enable users to retrieve details such as device version, interface status, or routing table information. For example, a playbook might first gather facts from a router to verify that it is running the correct version of IOS, and then proceed to apply a configuration update only if the device meets certain criteria. This dynamic approach to configuration management ensures that playbooks are flexible and adaptable to changing network conditions.

One of the main challenges of automating device configuration is dealing with device-specific differences. Although Ansible provides a set of standardized modules for different vendors, each vendor may implement certain features or configurations in slightly different ways. For example, the configuration syntax for interfaces may differ between Cisco IOS and Juniper Junos. To handle these differences, Ansible allows users to write conditional statements within playbooks. These conditionals can check for the device type or version and then apply vendor-specific configuration settings. This flexibility ensures that playbooks can be used across multi-vendor environments without needing to write separate playbooks for each device type.

Security is another important consideration when automating device configuration. Ansible provides tools to handle sensitive information, such as device credentials, securely. The ansible-vault feature allows users to encrypt sensitive data, such as passwords, so that they are not stored in plain text within playbooks or inventory files. This ensures that credentials are kept secure, even when sharing playbooks or working in a collaborative environment. Furthermore, Ansible's use of SSH for communication ensures that configuration changes are transmitted securely, reducing the risk of interception or unauthorized access.

Once the playbook is written and the inventory is defined, the final step is executing the playbook. Ansible provides a simple command-line interface for running playbooks, allowing users to specify which inventory to use and which playbook to execute. The ansible-playbook command initiates the playbook execution, and Ansible will automatically connect to the devices specified in the inventory, execute the tasks defined in the playbook, and report back the results. Any errors or issues that occur during execution are displayed in the output, providing valuable feedback for troubleshooting and refinement.

Automating device configuration with Ansible not only saves time but also improves the consistency and reliability of network configurations. By removing the need for manual intervention, network engineers can focus on higher-level tasks such as network design, optimization, and troubleshooting. The ability to quickly and efficiently apply configuration changes across multiple devices ensures that network environments remain up-to-date and secure. As networks continue to grow in complexity, tools like Ansible will play an increasingly important role in simplifying network management and enabling more agile, scalable infrastructures.

Chapter: Leveraging NETCONF for Network Device Management

In modern network management, the ability to effectively configure, monitor, and manage devices across a large infrastructure is essential. NETCONF (Network Configuration Protocol) has emerged as a powerful tool in this area, offering a standardized method for managing network devices and automating tasks. NETCONF provides an XML-based protocol designed to handle the configuration and retrieval of device states, offering a more structured and secure approach compared to traditional command-line interface (CLI) management. Understanding how to leverage NETCONF for network device management can help organizations streamline their network operations, reduce configuration errors, and increase the overall efficiency of network administration.

At its core, NETCONF is designed to provide a structured way of configuring network devices, such as routers, switches, and firewalls, by using XML data models to define configuration parameters and operations. Unlike traditional CLI management, which requires engineers to manually enter commands to configure devices, NETCONF allows for declarative configuration, where the desired end state is specified, and the protocol automatically ensures that the device is configured accordingly. This reduces the likelihood of human error and ensures consistency across a network.

To leverage NETCONF for network device management, the first step is to ensure that the network devices support the protocol. While many modern devices from major vendors like Cisco, Juniper, and Arista support NETCONF out of the box, it is important to verify that the device's firmware is compatible with the protocol and that the necessary services are enabled. For instance, on a Cisco IOS device, enabling NETCONF might involve configuring the device to accept NETCONF over SSH by running a specific command in the global configuration mode. Similarly, for Juniper devices running Junos OS, NETCONF can be enabled by configuring the system to listen for NETCONF requests over SSH. Once NETCONF is enabled, the device is ready to receive and respond to NETCONF requests, making it possible to automate configuration management.

The next step is to configure the NETCONF client, which is responsible for sending requests to the device and processing the responses. Ansible, for example, provides a set of modules that can be used to interact with NETCONF-enabled devices, allowing network engineers to automate the process of applying configurations and retrieving information. By using NETCONF in combination with Ansible, users can write playbooks to configure devices in a declarative manner, without having to worry about the intricacies of device-specific CLI commands. The Ansible netconf module allows for smooth communication between the client and the device, and it supports a variety of operations, including retrieving configuration data, applying changes, and even verifying the state of a device after modifications.

The ability to leverage NETCONF for network device management also offers significant advantages in terms of security and scalability. Traditional management methods, such as CLI, often rely on text-based protocols like SSH, which may expose sensitive configuration data if not properly secured. NETCONF, on the other hand, uses secure transport mechanisms like SSH or TLS to ensure that data is encrypted during transmission, reducing the risk of interception. Additionally, NETCONF supports role-based access control (RBAC) and other security features that can be configured to limit access to sensitive network configurations, providing more granular control over who can manage which devices and what actions they can perform.

Another key benefit of NETCONF is its ability to handle complex, hierarchical configurations. In large-scale networks, devices often have many layers of configurations, ranging from simple interface settings to complex routing and security policies. With NETCONF, these configurations can be represented in structured, XML-based data models, which makes it easier to automate complex tasks. For example, if an engineer needs to apply a series of VLAN configurations to multiple switches, NETCONF allows for the configuration data to be structured in a way that is consistent across all devices, ensuring that all switches are configured with the same settings. This can help eliminate discrepancies that might arise when manually configuring devices, ensuring that the network remains consistent and well-organized.

Moreover, NETCONF allows for real-time monitoring of network devices. With traditional CLI-based management, retrieving operational data often requires running commands manually on each device. NETCONF, however, allows users to query devices for specific operational data, such as interface status, routing table information, and system resource utilization. This capability makes it much easier to monitor the health of a network and identify potential issues before they become critical. For example, by using NETCONF to retrieve real-time interface statistics, engineers can quickly identify interfaces that are experiencing high utilization or errors, allowing them to take corrective action before network performance is impacted.

NETCONF also provides significant flexibility when it comes to device configuration and management. One of the primary challenges in network management is dealing with the variety of devices and configurations across an organization's infrastructure. Devices from different vendors, or even different models from the same vendor, can have varying command syntax and configuration methods. NETCONF, with its standard XML-based data models, provides a unified interface for interacting with devices from multiple vendors. By leveraging YANG models, a data modeling language used in conjunction with NETCONF, network engineers can define the structure of configuration data in a consistent way. YANG models abstract away the device-specific details, allowing engineers to focus on the configuration itself rather than the specific syntax required by each device.

Using YANG models with NETCONF also enables more advanced automation capabilities. YANG provides a machine-readable representation of configuration and operational data, which can be used to automate tasks such as configuration validation, change management, and even self-healing networks. For example, a network automation system could be set up to automatically validate the configuration of devices against predefined YANG models to ensure that they conform to organizational standards. If any discrepancies are found, the system could automatically trigger a remediation process to bring the device back into compliance. This level of automation can significantly reduce the workload of network administrators and improve the overall reliability of the network.

The flexibility and scalability of NETCONF make it an ideal solution for managing large and complex networks. As organizations expand their infrastructures and introduce more devices, manual configuration and management become increasingly impractical. NETCONF provides a scalable and efficient way to manage a growing network, allowing administrators to automate configuration changes, monitor device states, and ensure consistency across the entire infrastructure. Whether it's applying security patches, configuring interfaces, or troubleshooting issues, NETCONF offers a standardized method for managing network devices that simplifies the process and improves overall efficiency.

Leveraging NETCONF for network device management also fosters better collaboration and integration within IT teams. Because NETCONF operates on an open standard, it can easily be integrated with other network management tools and platforms. This enables cross-platform automation and orchestration, allowing network engineers to build more sophisticated workflows and integrate NETCONF with other systems, such as network monitoring platforms, ticketing systems, and cloud management tools. This level of integration is essential for building modern, agile network infrastructures that can quickly adapt to changing business needs.

By adopting NETCONF for network device management, organizations can greatly enhance their ability to manage complex, distributed networks. The protocol's ability to standardize device configuration and management, improve security, and enable automation makes it a powerful tool in the modern network engineer's toolkit. As networks continue to grow in complexity, leveraging NETCONF for device management will become an increasingly important part of network operations.

Chapter: Understanding the NETCONF Protocol

NETCONF (Network Configuration Protocol) is a powerful and flexible protocol designed for managing and automating network devices. It offers a standardized approach to network configuration, monitoring, and management, addressing the limitations of traditional CLI-based configuration methods. As networks become more complex and diverse, the need for an efficient, reliable, and scalable configuration management system grows. NETCONF addresses this challenge by providing a structured and secure way to manage network devices through XML-based data models. Understanding the NETCONF protocol is essential for network engineers looking to automate configuration tasks, improve network consistency, and streamline operations across a wide variety of devices and vendors.

At its core, NETCONF is designed to manage the configuration and state of network devices in a way that is both secure and efficient. Unlike traditional methods that require manual entry of configuration commands through a device's CLI, NETCONF allows users to define and manage configurations in a standardized format. This makes it easier to automate the process of applying, updating, and verifying configurations on network devices. NETCONF's use of XML as the data format allows for rich, structured configurations, which are easier to parse and manipulate programmatically. This structured approach to configuration is a major advantage over traditional text-based configurations, which can be error-prone and difficult to manage in large, dynamic networks.

One of the key features of the NETCONF protocol is its ability to interact with network devices in a vendor-agnostic manner. Traditional CLI-based management is often specific to a particular vendor or device model, meaning that network engineers must learn and adapt to the idiosyncrasies of different devices. NETCONF, on the other hand, provides a unified interface for managing devices from different vendors, abstracting away the device-specific details. By using a common set of operations and data models, NETCONF allows network engineers to interact with a wide variety of devices in a consistent manner, making it easier to manage complex, multi-vendor networks.

NETCONF operates over transport protocols such as SSH (Secure Shell), which ensures secure communication between the client and the device. This makes NETCONF more secure than traditional CLI methods, which may not always use encryption or secure authentication mechanisms. The use of SSH as the transport protocol provides encryption for both the configuration data and any authentication credentials, protecting sensitive information during transmission. Additionally, NETCONF supports role-based access control (RBAC), which allows administrators to define granular permissions for users, further enhancing the security of the network management process.

The protocol itself is composed of several key operations that allow network engineers to manage device configurations. These operations include the ability to get, edit, and delete configuration data, as well as to commit or roll back changes. The most common operations are get-config, edit-config, and commit. The get-config operation allows users to retrieve the current configuration of a device, while the edit-config operation is used to modify or add new configuration settings. The commit operation applies the changes to the device, ensuring that the configuration is written to memory and becomes active. Additionally, NETCONF supports validate and copy-config operations, which are useful for ensuring that configurations are valid before applying them and for managing backup configurations.

Another important feature of NETCONF is its support for data modeling through YANG (Yet Another Next Generation). YANG is a data modeling language used to define the structure and semantics of configuration and operational data on network devices. YANG models provide a standardized way to represent device configurations, making it easier to automate configuration management and ensure consistency across devices. With YANG, users can define the allowed configuration parameters, constraints, and default values for each device, ensuring that configurations are applied correctly and consistently. YANG models also allow for more sophisticated operations, such as validation and error checking, which further enhance the reliability and robustness of the network configuration process.

NETCONF's use of YANG models is particularly beneficial in environments with multiple vendors or device types. In traditional CLI-based management, each vendor often defines its own configuration syntax and parameters, making it difficult to manage configurations across devices from different vendors. With YANG, however, the data model defines a standardized structure for configuration data, which can be applied consistently across devices from different vendors. This abstraction layer simplifies the configuration process and reduces the complexity associated with managing multi-vendor networks. Additionally, by using YANG models, network engineers can write more flexible and reusable automation scripts, as the same model can be applied to different devices, regardless of the underlying hardware.

NETCONF also supports transactional operations, which allow users to make configuration changes in a safe and reliable manner. Transactions ensure that changes are only applied if all operations in a sequence are successful. If any operation fails, the entire transaction can be rolled back, preserving the integrity of the device's configuration. This capability is particularly useful in complex environments where multiple changes need to be applied in a single session, as it guarantees that the device will either be fully updated or remain in its previous stable state. This transactional approach eliminates the risk of partial configurations, which could result in network outages or other issues.

Additionally, NETCONF provides real-time monitoring capabilities, allowing network engineers to retrieve operational data from devices. This can include information about the status of network interfaces, routing tables, device health, and other performance metrics. By using NETCONF to gather operational data, network engineers can monitor the state of the network and quickly identify potential issues. This is especially valuable in large networks, where manually checking the status of each device would be time-consuming and impractical. The ability to automate data retrieval and monitoring makes NETCONF an essential tool for proactive network management.

Another important aspect of NETCONF is its extensibility. The protocol allows for the addition of custom operations and features, enabling network engineers to tailor the protocol to their specific needs. This flexibility allows NETCONF to evolve alongside changing network requirements, ensuring that it remains relevant as new technologies and devices are introduced. As the network landscape continues to evolve, NETCONF's ability to integrate with other systems and support custom extensions will ensure that it remains a valuable tool for network automation and management.

Understanding the NETCONF protocol is essential for network engineers seeking to automate and streamline their device management processes. NETCONF's secure, standardized approach to configuration management, coupled with its support for data modeling and real-time monitoring, makes it an ideal choice for managing complex, multi-vendor networks. By leveraging NETCONF, organizations can improve the consistency, security, and efficiency of their network operations, ultimately enabling more agile and scalable network management. As the demand for automation and orchestration continues to grow, NETCONF will play an increasingly important role in the evolution of network management practices.

Chapter: YANG Models and Their Role in Network Automation

In the realm of network automation, managing configurations and ensuring consistency across diverse devices is essential for efficient and scalable operations. One of the most powerful tools for achieving this is YANG (Yet Another Next Generation), a data modeling language that plays a pivotal role in network automation. YANG provides a standardized way to represent configuration and operational data for network devices, making it easier to automate the management of network infrastructure. By defining a clear, structured representation of network configurations, YANG helps network engineers automate the deployment, validation, and monitoring of network devices while maintaining consistency across complex, multi-vendor environments.

YANG models define the structure and semantics of the data used to configure network devices. They act as blueprints for device configuration and state information, specifying what parameters can be configured, their types, constraints, and relationships. YANG is used in conjunction with NETCONF, a network management protocol, to define and manipulate these configurations on devices. The use of YANG models ensures that configurations are standardized across devices and that network engineers can apply consistent policies, regardless of the vendor or device type. This abstraction layer simplifies the task of network management by eliminating the need to understand each device's proprietary configuration language and syntax.

The role of YANG models in network automation is particularly critical when managing multi-vendor networks. In traditional network management, each device vendor often has its own proprietary configuration syntax and command set, which can make it challenging to automate configuration tasks. YANG provides a uniform representation of configuration data, which can be used across devices from different vendors. This standardization reduces the complexity of managing a diverse set of network devices, as network engineers can work with a common data model instead of needing to learn and adapt to each device's unique configuration language. With YANG, a single automation script can be written to manage configurations across various devices, making it easier to scale automation efforts across large, complex networks.

In network automation, YANG models are used to define not only configuration parameters but also the operational state of devices. Network engineers can use YANG to specify what data is available for monitoring, such as interface status, routing table information, and device health. This ability to define both configuration and operational data is crucial for network monitoring and troubleshooting. By using YANG models to retrieve operational data, network engineers can quickly assess the health of their network, identify potential issues, and take corrective action before problems escalate. For instance, a YANG model might define the structure for retrieving interface statistics or monitoring the performance of a network device, allowing network engineers to automate the collection and analysis of real-time data across their infrastructure.

One of the primary advantages of using YANG models in network automation is their flexibility. YANG allows for the definition of custom data models that can be tailored to meet the specific needs of a network. Network engineers can extend YANG models to include additional parameters or configurations that are unique to their network or use case. This extensibility makes YANG highly adaptable and capable of supporting a wide range of devices, from routers and switches to firewalls and load balancers. As network environments evolve and new technologies emerge, YANG models can be extended or modified to accommodate new requirements, ensuring that network automation efforts remain relevant and effective over time.

YANG also facilitates the validation of configurations before they are applied to devices. By defining the constraints and acceptable values for configuration parameters, YANG helps ensure that only valid configurations are deployed. For example, a YANG model can specify that an IP address must be within a certain range or that an interface must support a specific type of protocol. This built-in validation reduces the risk of configuration errors and ensures that network devices are consistently configured according to predefined standards. Additionally, YANG models can be used to validate existing configurations, ensuring that devices remain in compliance with organizational policies and standards.

In addition to configuration management, YANG models are integral to the concept of network programmability. By providing a standardized representation of network configurations, YANG enables network devices to be managed through software-driven approaches, such as network automation tools and orchestration platforms. Network programmability allows network engineers to automate tasks such as provisioning new devices, configuring network services, and applying security policies. With YANG, the automation process becomes more reliable and efficient, as network engineers can focus on defining high-level policies rather than dealing with the complexities of individual device configurations. This programmability also supports the dynamic nature of modern networks, where changes must be applied quickly and consistently across a large number of devices.

The integration of YANG models with network automation tools like Ansible, Chef, and Puppet has made it easier to automate and scale network management tasks. These tools use YANG models as a foundation for managing network devices, providing a common language for automation. For example, Ansible's netconf module supports the use of YANG models to configure devices over NETCONF, enabling network engineers to automate tasks such as configuring interfaces, setting up routing protocols, and applying security policies. This integration allows for seamless automation workflows, where YANG models serve as the bridge between the desired configuration and the actual device state. By incorporating YANG into network automation platforms, engineers can achieve greater consistency, reduce errors, and improve the overall efficiency of their network operations.

YANG models also support the concept of network state monitoring and verification. In addition to defining configuration parameters, YANG models specify the operational state of devices, such as interface statistics and performance metrics. This information can be used to monitor the health and performance of a network in real-time, providing network engineers with the data needed to make informed decisions. By integrating YANG with monitoring tools, engineers can automate the collection and analysis of operational data, helping to identify issues early and ensure that the network is performing optimally.

As networks continue to grow in complexity and scale, the role of YANG models in network automation will only become more important. YANG provides a powerful and flexible framework for managing network configurations, ensuring that devices are consistently configured and monitored according to predefined standards. With the ability to define custom models, validate configurations, and integrate with automation tools, YANG is essential for enabling efficient and scalable network management. As organizations embrace automation and seek to optimize their network operations, YANG models will play a central role in transforming how networks are managed and operated, making them more agile, secure, and efficient.

Chapter: NETCONF and Ansible Integration

The combination of NETCONF and Ansible offers a powerful approach to network automation, providing network engineers with the ability to automate configuration management, monitoring, and operational tasks across a variety of network devices. NETCONF, a network configuration protocol, enables structured communication with network devices, allowing users to define, retrieve, and manage configurations in a standardized manner. Ansible, a widely used automation platform, complements NETCONF by enabling the automation of tasks such as configuration deployment, device management, and data retrieval. By integrating NETCONF with Ansible, network administrators can streamline network management tasks, reduce human error, and improve the overall efficiency of network operations.

NETCONF provides a standardized protocol for managing network devices, offering a more structured and secure alternative to traditional command-line interface (CLI) management. It uses XML-based data models to represent configuration and operational data, ensuring that network devices can be managed in a consistent and vendor-agnostic manner. However, while NETCONF provides the underlying protocol for network device management, Ansible adds a layer of automation and orchestration, enabling users to define and execute complex workflows for managing network devices at scale. By integrating NETCONF with Ansible, users can benefit from a unified approach to network management, where NETCONF handles device configuration and state management, while Ansible orchestrates tasks and automates workflows.

One of the primary benefits of integrating NETCONF with Ansible is the ability to automate complex network configurations in a repeatable and reliable manner. Ansible's declarative approach to automation allows users to define the desired state of a network device, and NETCONF ensures that the device configuration matches that state. For example, an Ansible playbook can be used to automate the configuration of network interfaces, routing protocols, or security policies across a variety of devices. The netconf module in Ansible allows users to interact with NETCONF-enabled devices and apply configurations defined in the playbook. This integration eliminates the need for manual configuration of each device, reducing the risk of errors and ensuring that the network remains consistent and properly configured.

The integration between NETCONF and Ansible is particularly valuable in multi-vendor network environments, where devices from different manufacturers are deployed. Traditional network management methods often require engineers to learn the specific CLI syntax for each vendor, making it difficult to manage a heterogeneous network. NETCONF, however, abstracts the device-specific details and provides a unified interface for interacting with devices from different vendors. Ansible's ability to use NETCONF modules allows engineers to write playbooks that can be executed on a wide range of devices, regardless of the manufacturer. This simplifies network management by enabling network engineers to automate tasks across multi-vendor environments without needing to deal with the complexities of different device configurations.

In addition to simplifying device configuration, integrating NETCONF with Ansible also enhances the ability to collect operational data from devices. NETCONF's get-config and get operations allow users to retrieve configuration data and operational state information from network devices, such as interface statistics, routing tables, and system health metrics. Ansible can use these NETCONF operations to gather real-time data from devices and make decisions based on that information. For example, Ansible playbooks can be written to check the status of network interfaces across multiple devices, gather performance metrics, and trigger alerts or corrective actions if certain thresholds are exceeded. This integration allows for proactive network management, as engineers can automate both configuration management and monitoring tasks within the same workflow.

Another key advantage of NETCONF and Ansible integration is the ability to validate configurations before they are applied to network devices. Ansible provides the ability to include conditional logic and validation steps within playbooks, ensuring that configurations are only applied when certain conditions are met. NETCONF's structured data format makes it easier to validate configuration parameters before they are pushed to devices, ensuring that the desired state is reached without causing disruptions or misconfigurations. For example, Ansible playbooks can check whether a router's interface is already configured with a specific IP address before applying a new configuration, preventing unnecessary changes and reducing the risk of downtime.

The combination of NETCONF and Ansible also facilitates the use of role-based access control (RBAC) to secure device configurations. NETCONF supports RBAC, allowing administrators to control which users or systems have access to specific configuration data and operations. Ansible's integration with NETCONF can take advantage of these security features by enforcing access control policies when automating configuration changes. This ensures that only authorized users or systems can make changes to critical network configurations, helping to protect the network from unauthorized access or accidental misconfigurations.

Furthermore, integrating NETCONF with Ansible provides significant advantages when it comes to automation at scale. In large networks with hundreds or thousands of devices, manually configuring or monitoring devices becomes increasingly impractical. Ansible's ability to define inventory files and apply playbooks to groups of devices enables network engineers to manage large-scale networks efficiently. By leveraging NETCONF's structured configuration model, Ansible can automate the application of configuration changes across thousands of devices with a single command, ensuring consistency and reducing the time required to make changes. Whether applying a firmware update, modifying routing policies, or reconfiguring interfaces, this integration enables network engineers to scale automation efforts across complex infrastructures.

NETCONF and Ansible also provide flexibility in managing network configurations across both physical and virtual environments. With the rise of network virtualization and software-defined networking (SDN), managing virtual network devices has become an increasingly important aspect of network automation. NETCONF, in combination with Ansible, offers the flexibility to manage both physical devices, such as routers and switches, as well as virtual network elements, such as virtual routers or network functions. By using NETCONF to configure virtual devices and Ansible to orchestrate tasks across both physical and virtual networks, network engineers can maintain a unified approach to managing their entire infrastructure, regardless of whether the devices are physical or virtual.

The integration of NETCONF and Ansible also facilitates the adoption of more advanced automation workflows, such as network intent-based automation. In intent-based networking, network engineers define high-level policies or intents, and the automation system translates these intents into specific configuration changes on devices. By using NETCONF as the protocol for managing configurations and Ansible for orchestrating automation workflows, engineers can create intelligent, intent-driven networks that automatically adapt to changing business needs. This approach to network automation reduces the complexity of manual configuration and ensures that the network can evolve dynamically based on the needs of the organization.

As organizations continue to adopt automation and orchestration as part of their network management strategies, the integration of NETCONF with Ansible provides a robust solution for managing and automating network configurations at scale. The combination of NETCONF's structured data models and Ansible's powerful automation capabilities allows network engineers to automate both configuration management and monitoring tasks, ensuring consistency, reducing errors, and improving overall network performance. By streamlining network management processes, this integration enables organizations to build more agile, scalable, and secure network infrastructures.

Chapter: Managing Network Devices with NETCONF and Ansible

The management of network devices is a fundamental aspect of network administration, and as networks grow in complexity, the need for efficient, scalable, and automated solutions becomes more critical. NETCONF, or Network Configuration Protocol, combined with Ansible, a popular automation tool, offers a powerful and flexible way to automate the management of network devices. This integration enables network engineers to automate configuration tasks, retrieve operational data, and ensure that devices remain consistent with organizational policies. By using NETCONF and Ansible together, network administrators can reduce manual effort, minimize errors, and improve overall network performance and reliability.

NETCONF is a protocol designed for network management, providing a secure and structured way to configure network devices and retrieve operational data. Unlike traditional CLI-based management, which can be device-specific and error-prone, NETCONF uses standardized XML data models to represent configuration and operational data. This makes it easier for network engineers to manage devices across different vendors in a uniform way. NETCONF supports several key operations such as get-config for retrieving configurations, edit-config for applying changes, and commit for finalizing configuration updates. These operations allow network administrators to manage devices in a more predictable and controlled manner, ensuring that configuration changes are applied correctly and consistently.

Ansible, on the other hand, is a powerful automation tool that simplifies IT tasks by allowing users to define and execute workflows in a declarative way. Through Ansible, network engineers can write playbooks to automate network configuration, retrieve device data, and perform routine tasks like updating firmware or applying security patches. Ansible's playbooks are written in YAML, a human-readable format, which makes them easy to write, maintain, and understand. With its vast collection of modules, Ansible can work with a variety of devices and protocols, including NETCONF. The integration of NETCONF and Ansible enables engineers to manage network devices with ease, applying configurations and retrieving data without the need for manual intervention.

By combining NETCONF's structured configuration management with Ansible's automation capabilities, network engineers can build powerful workflows that simplify network management. The process begins with defining an inventory, which specifies the devices that Ansible will manage. The inventory can be a static file listing IP addresses, or it can be dynamic, pulling device information from external systems. Once the inventory is set, engineers can write Ansible playbooks to target specific devices or groups of devices and apply the desired configurations. Ansible's netconf module provides the interface to interact with NETCONF-enabled devices, making it possible to configure devices, retrieve data, and perform other management tasks.

One of the key advantages of using NETCONF and Ansible together is the ability to automate complex configuration tasks that would otherwise require manual intervention. For example, configuring network interfaces, routing protocols, or applying security policies across multiple devices can be time-consuming and error-prone when done manually. By writing Ansible playbooks that use NETCONF modules, network engineers can ensure that configurations are applied consistently across devices. This automation helps reduce the risk of human error, ensures that devices are properly configured, and speeds up the process of applying changes across large networks.

Another benefit of managing network devices with NETCONF and Ansible is the ability to collect operational data from devices in real-time. NETCONF allows engineers to retrieve device status information such as interface statistics, routing table entries, and system health metrics. Ansible can use NETCONF to collect this data and incorporate it into automation workflows. For example, Ansible playbooks can be written to check the status of network interfaces across multiple devices and take action if any interfaces are down or experiencing high traffic. This proactive monitoring allows network engineers to identify issues before they escalate and take corrective action to prevent network outages or performance degradation.

NETCONF's ability to manage network devices in a vendor-agnostic manner makes it especially useful in multi-vendor environments. Traditional network management tools often require engineers to learn the specific command syntax for each device vendor, which can be time-consuming and difficult to manage at scale. NETCONF eliminates this challenge by providing a unified interface for interacting with devices from different manufacturers. Ansible's integration with NETCONF further simplifies this process by allowing engineers to write playbooks that work across multiple devices, regardless of the vendor. This standardization makes it easier to automate network management tasks and ensures that configurations are applied consistently across the entire infrastructure.

The integration of NETCONF and Ansible also provides greater flexibility in managing network devices. Ansible allows users to define variables and conditional logic within playbooks, enabling engineers to customize automation workflows based on device-specific requirements. For instance, variables can be defined for device IP addresses, usernames, passwords, and other configuration parameters, making it possible to reuse the same playbook across different devices and environments. Additionally, Ansible's ability to handle loops and conditionals allows for more complex workflows, such as applying different configurations based on device role or status.

Another important aspect of NETCONF and Ansible integration is the ability to validate configurations before applying them to devices. Configuration validation ensures that the changes being made are correct and will not disrupt network operations. Ansible's support for validation tasks allows network engineers to check whether the desired configuration is already in place before making changes. For example, a playbook could first retrieve the current configuration of a device using NETCONF, compare it to the desired configuration, and only apply the changes if the device is not already configured as required. This validation process helps prevent errors and ensures that configuration changes are applied safely and efficiently.

Security is another key consideration when managing network devices with NETCONF and Ansible. NETCONF supports secure communication over protocols like SSH or TLS, which ensures that sensitive configuration data is encrypted during transmission.

Additionally, NETCONF supports role-based access control (RBAC), which allows administrators to define which users or systems can access specific configuration data and perform certain operations. Ansible's integration with NETCONF respects these security settings, ensuring that only authorized users can execute playbooks that modify network configurations. This helps safeguard the network from unauthorized access and accidental misconfigurations.

As networks continue to grow in complexity and scale, managing network devices manually becomes increasingly impractical. The integration of NETCONF and Ansible provides a solution that allows network engineers to automate configuration management, data retrieval, and monitoring tasks across a variety of devices. By using NETCONF to standardize device configurations and Ansible to orchestrate automation workflows, network engineers can achieve greater efficiency, reduce errors, and improve the overall reliability of the network. The combination of these two technologies provides a flexible, scalable, and secure solution for managing modern networks, making it easier to handle the demands of complex, multi-vendor environments.

Chapter: Writing Custom NETCONF Modules for Ansible

The ability to extend Ansible's functionality with custom modules is one of the reasons why it is such a powerful tool for automating network management. NETCONF, the network configuration protocol, plays a critical role in network automation, providing a standardized method for configuring network devices and retrieving operational data. While Ansible includes a variety of modules that work with NETCONF-enabled devices, there are scenarios where off-the-shelf modules do not meet the specific needs of a network environment. In such cases, writing custom NETCONF modules for Ansible becomes an essential skill. Custom modules allow network engineers to tailor the automation process to their specific requirements, ensuring that Ansible can interface seamlessly with a wide range of network devices and configurations.

Ansible modules are small, reusable pieces of code that interact with systems, applications, or network devices to perform tasks such as configuration management, monitoring, or querying system state. NETCONF modules, in particular, are responsible for facilitating communication with devices that support the NETCONF protocol. These modules can send requests to devices, retrieve configuration or operational data, and apply changes based on predefined configurations. Writing custom NETCONF modules for Ansible provides the flexibility to interact with devices in ways that might not be supported by the existing set of modules, enabling network engineers to automate tasks that are specific to their network's needs.

The first step in writing a custom NETCONF module for Ansible is to understand the basic structure and workflow of how Ansible interacts with devices using NETCONF. NETCONF uses XML to represent configuration data and operations, so the custom module must be capable of constructing, sending, and parsing XML data in a way that is compatible with the NETCONF protocol. The module must also handle communication with the NETCONF server, which typically happens over secure transport protocols like SSH or TLS. Ansible provides a framework for writing custom modules, allowing developers to integrate the module seamlessly into Ansible's automation workflows.

To begin writing a custom NETCONF module, it is important to have a strong understanding of the NETCONF protocol itself. The NETCONF protocol defines several core operations, such as get-config, edit-config, commit, and validate. Each of these operations interacts with network devices differently and requires different types of XML data. For instance, the get-config operation is used to retrieve the current configuration from a device, while edit-config is used to apply changes to the configuration. The custom module must be able to handle these operations, ensuring that they are properly constructed, sent to the device, and parsed in response.

Ansible provides a Python-based framework for writing custom modules, and the NETCONF-specific functionality is typically built using libraries such as ncclient. ncclient is a Python library that simplifies the process of interacting with NETCONF-enabled devices, providing a high-level API for sending NETCONF operations and receiving responses. By using ncclient, developers can focus on writing the logic for the module rather than having to deal with the low-level details of XML handling and NETCONF communication. The custom module must be written in such a way that it can handle different device configurations, retrieve relevant data, and apply the necessary changes.

The next step is to define the module's parameters and functionality. Custom NETCONF modules for Ansible need to specify what data the module will accept from the user, such as the target device's IP address, username, password, and any other parameters required for communication. This might include details like the NETCONF operation to be performed, the specific XML configuration to be applied, or the operational data to be queried. The module should also define the expected behavior, including how it will process the results and handle errors. For example, a module that retrieves configuration data might output the result as a structured dictionary, while a module that modifies configurations may provide feedback indicating whether the operation was successful or if there were any errors.

Once the custom NETCONF module is written, it can be tested using Ansible's built-in testing framework. Ansible allows users to write test cases for custom modules, ensuring that the module behaves as expected in different scenarios. Testing the module is essential to verify that it interacts correctly with the target device, handles errors gracefully, and provides accurate feedback to the user. It is also important to test the module in various environments, as different devices may have unique requirements or constraints that must be considered. By thoroughly testing the custom module, network engineers can ensure that it will function reliably when deployed in production.

Ansible's integration with Python makes writing custom NETCONF modules accessible even for network engineers who may not have extensive software development experience. The use of ncclient and other Python libraries allows developers to leverage existing tools while focusing on the higher-level functionality required for network automation. Custom modules can be written to handle specific tasks, such as configuring VLANs, applying security policies, or retrieving operational data, and can be integrated into Ansible playbooks just like any other module.

One of the advantages of writing custom NETCONF modules for Ansible is that it allows for greater flexibility and scalability in network automation. While Ansible's existing NETCONF modules cover a wide range of common tasks, custom modules can be written to address the unique needs of an organization's network. For example, if a particular vendor's NETCONF implementation has custom extensions or non-standard features, a custom module can be developed to interact with those features. Custom modules can also handle complex workflows that involve multiple NETCONF operations or integrate with other automation tools and platforms.

Another key advantage of custom NETCONF modules is the ability to integrate them with existing automation pipelines and tools. Once the custom module is developed, it can be reused in multiple playbooks, enabling network engineers to automate repetitive tasks across large-scale networks. The ability to define and reuse custom modules makes it easier to maintain consistent configurations across the network, ensuring that devices are properly configured and monitored. By writing modular code that can be reused and adapted as needed, network engineers can improve the efficiency and effectiveness of their automation workflows.

Security is an important consideration when writing custom NETCONF modules, as these modules will be interacting with network devices that may store sensitive configuration data. It is crucial to ensure that the communication between Ansible and the network devices is secure, using encryption and secure authentication methods like SSH or TLS. Additionally, custom modules must handle sensitive data, such as device credentials or configuration parameters, securely. Ansible's built-in support for encryption and secure authentication methods can be leveraged to ensure that network devices are managed in a secure manner.

By writing custom NETCONF modules for Ansible, network engineers can take full control over the automation of network device management, enabling them to streamline workflows, ensure consistency, and improve the efficiency of network operations. The ability to tailor NETCONF interactions to the specific needs of an organization's network allows for greater flexibility and scalability, making it easier to manage complex infrastructures. As networks continue to evolve and become more dynamic, the development of custom NETCONF modules will play an increasingly important role in the automation of network management tasks.

Chapter: Automating Network Device Backups

Network device backups are a crucial part of network management, ensuring that configurations and data can be restored in case of failure or disaster. Traditionally, network engineers would manually back up configurations from devices such as routers, switches, and firewalls by logging into each device and executing backup commands. While effective, this process can be time-consuming, prone to human error, and difficult to scale in larger network environments. Automation, however, offers a much more efficient and reliable solution. By automating network device backups, network administrators can ensure that their devices are consistently backed up, configurations are easily recoverable, and network downtime is minimized.

Automating network device backups begins with defining the backup process itself. Typically, a network device backup involves retrieving the running configuration, storing it securely, and verifying that the backup was successful. In large networks with many devices, this task becomes increasingly cumbersome when done manually. By automating the backup process, network engineers can ensure that backups are performed regularly and that the correct configuration files are stored. This reduces the risk of losing critical configurations and improves the overall resilience of the network.

One of the most effective ways to automate network device backups is by using network automation tools like Ansible, which integrates with various protocols, including SSH and NETCONF, to interact with network devices. Ansible's playbooks, written in YAML, allow network engineers to define automated tasks in a human-readable format. By leveraging the power of Ansible modules, such as ios_config for Cisco devices or junos_config for Juniper devices, network engineers can create playbooks that retrieve and store device configurations automatically. These playbooks can be scheduled to run at regular intervals, ensuring that the network devices are always backed up without manual intervention.

Ansible's flexibility also allows for the use of dynamic inventory, which is useful in larger networks where the number of devices may change frequently. Instead of manually updating inventory files whenever a new device is added, dynamic inventory allows Ansible to query an external source, such as a cloud management platform or a network monitoring tool, to gather the list of devices to be backed up. This ensures that the backup process is always up to date, even as devices are added or removed from the network.

The backup process typically involves connecting to each network device and running a series of commands to retrieve the device's configuration. For instance, a backup of a Cisco router might involve executing the show running-config command, which outputs the device's current configuration. In an automated backup system, Ansible can send these commands via SSH to the devices and capture the output. The retrieved configuration is then saved to a secure location, such as a file server, cloud storage, or version-controlled repository, where it can be easily accessed in case a restoration is needed.

The scheduling of backups is another important consideration. In traditional manual backup processes, the frequency of backups often depends on the administrator's discretion, and it's easy to forget or delay backups. By automating backups with tools like Ansible, network engineers can set up a fixed schedule for regular backups, ensuring that configurations are backed up at intervals that align with organizational policies or compliance requirements. This schedule can be customized to run daily, weekly, or monthly, depending on the criticality of the devices and the rate at which their configurations change.

Security is a critical aspect of automating network device backups. Configuration files often contain sensitive information, such as passwords, routing policies, and security settings, which must be protected from unauthorized access. Ansible's integration with security tools like Ansible Vault can help secure backup files by encrypting sensitive data during storage. Ansible Vault ensures that even if a backup file is compromised, the sensitive information it contains is not easily accessible without the proper decryption key. Additionally, secure transport protocols such as SSH should be used to ensure that the backup process is encrypted during transmission, preventing unauthorized access to configuration data while it is being transferred.

The ability to verify backup success is another benefit of automation. In a manual backup process, it's easy to overlook whether a backup was completed successfully. By automating backups, Ansible can be configured to verify whether the backup process completed successfully and alert network engineers in case of any issues. For instance, after each backup task, a playbook can include checks to verify that the correct configuration file was saved, and if the file is missing or corrupted, the automation system can send an alert to the network administrator for further investigation. This automated verification process ensures that backups are not only taken regularly but also that they are complete and accurate.

In addition to regular backups, it's important to consider the storage and retention of backup files. For example, older backups that are no longer necessary could be automatically deleted to free up storage space. Ansible playbooks can be written to manage backup retention policies, ensuring that only the most recent or most relevant backups are kept and older ones are archived or deleted. This ensures that backup storage is managed efficiently and that there is always enough space for new backups without overburdening the storage system.

When network devices experience configuration changes, whether due to updates, new policies, or troubleshooting, it's crucial to update the backups accordingly. By automating backups, every time a change is made to a device, the configuration is captured and stored, ensuring that the most current version of the device's configuration is always available for restoration. This is particularly important in environments where configurations change frequently, and the backup process needs to be kept in sync with those changes.

Another useful feature of automating network device backups is the ability to keep backup files version-controlled. Ansible, in combination with a version control system such as Git, allows backup files to be tracked over time. This gives network engineers the ability to see the history of configuration changes, compare different versions of a configuration, and roll back to a previous configuration if necessary. This version control mechanism provides a valuable audit trail, which can be useful for troubleshooting, compliance reporting, or disaster recovery.

Automating network device backups not only improves the reliability and efficiency of network management but also enhances the overall security and disaster recovery capabilities of an organization. By automating the process, network engineers can ensure that backups are taken regularly, stored securely, and are easily accessible when needed. The use of tools like Ansible provides the flexibility to scale the backup process across a large number of devices, even in complex, multi-vendor environments. As networks continue to grow and evolve, automated backup systems will become increasingly important in maintaining the availability and integrity of network configurations, ensuring that organizations are prepared for any eventuality.

Chapter: Handling Error Management in Ansible for Network Tasks

Error management is a critical aspect of any network automation process, as network environments are inherently dynamic and can be prone to disruptions caused by misconfigurations, connectivity issues, or device failures. In Ansible, error management plays a significant role in ensuring that automation tasks are executed reliably and in a controlled manner. When automating network tasks, network engineers need to ensure that errors are detected promptly, handled appropriately, and that recovery mechanisms are in place to minimize the impact of failures. By using Ansible's built-in error management features and customizing workflows to account for specific network environments, engineers can significantly improve the reliability and stability of their automation processes.

Ansible's error management capabilities are centered around the concept of task execution. In a typical Ansible playbook, tasks are defined to perform various actions, such as configuring devices, gathering data, or applying updates. Each task is executed sequentially, and Ansible provides feedback on whether the task was successful or failed. In network automation, failures can be caused by a variety of issues, such as network connectivity problems, misconfigured devices, or even incorrect parameters. Ansible's robust error handling mechanisms help ensure that errors are caught, handled gracefully, and that network engineers are notified of any issues that arise during execution.

One of the primary tools for handling errors in Ansible is the failed state, which is triggered when a task does not complete successfully. By default, Ansible will stop executing the playbook when a task fails, which ensures that no further configuration changes are made if an error occurs. However, in many cases, it may be preferable to allow the playbook to continue executing even when certain tasks fail. This can be useful in situations where some failures are non-critical, and network engineers want the automation process to complete as much of the work as possible. To handle such scenarios, Ansible provides the ignore_errors directive, which allows tasks to fail without halting the entire playbook. By using this directive, engineers can ensure that non-critical errors do not prevent other tasks from executing.

In addition to ignore_errors, Ansible offers the ability to handle errors using the block, rescue, and always directives. These directives provide more granular control over how tasks are executed and how errors are handled. A block is a group of tasks that are executed together. If one of the tasks in the block fails, the playbook will proceed to the rescue section, where a different set of tasks can be defined to handle the error, such as rolling back changes or sending alerts. The always directive ensures that certain tasks are always executed, regardless of whether previous tasks succeed or fail. This is useful for tasks that should run as a cleanup step, such as closing connections or logging error details. By using these directives, network engineers can create more sophisticated error management workflows that allow for greater control over how errors are handled in different parts of the playbook.

When dealing with network tasks, it is also important to consider network-specific errors, such as device unavailability, connection timeouts, or authentication failures. Ansible provides the retries and delay options, which allow users to implement retry logic when interacting with network devices. For example, if an Ansible playbook is trying to configure a device and encounters a timeout error, the retries and delay options can be used to retry the task a specified number of times with a delay between each attempt. This is particularly useful when dealing with network devices that may experience temporary outages or slow response times. By implementing retries, network engineers can ensure that their automation tasks are more resilient and can recover from transient network issues without requiring manual intervention.

Ansible's when conditional statement can also be used to handle errors more dynamically by allowing tasks to be executed only under certain conditions. For instance, a task that configures a device could be set to run only if the device is reachable, as determined by a previous task that checks network connectivity. This ensures that tasks are only executed when the necessary prerequisites are met, preventing errors that might arise from attempting to configure a device that is offline or unreachable. The when statement allows Ansible to adapt to changing network conditions, ensuring that errors are avoided before they can occur.

Another important aspect of error management is logging. Ansible provides several options for logging task output, including verbosity levels and the ability to capture specific error messages. By increasing the verbosity of the playbook output, engineers can get more detailed information about the specific errors that occurred during execution. Ansible also supports redirecting output to log files, making it easier to track and analyze errors over time. By analyzing these logs, network engineers can identify recurring issues, troubleshoot problems more effectively, and make informed decisions about improving the network automation process.

In addition to logging and handling specific errors, it is also important to consider the overall monitoring and alerting aspects of network automation. Ansible can be integrated with external monitoring systems, such as Nagios or Zabbix, to provide real-time alerts when errors occur during automation tasks. These systems can monitor the status of playbook executions and notify network engineers when tasks fail, enabling them to take immediate corrective action. Integrating Ansible with a monitoring platform ensures that errors are detected and addressed in a timely manner, minimizing downtime and preventing configuration drift in the network.

When writing playbooks for network tasks, engineers should also consider implementing fallback mechanisms to ensure that errors are handled in a way that minimizes the impact on the network. For example, if a playbook is intended to apply a configuration change to multiple devices, but one of the devices fails, the playbook could be written to skip that device and continue with the rest. This ensures that the other devices are still configured as expected, and the failed device can be addressed separately. Fallback mechanisms help maintain the integrity of the network while ensuring that tasks are completed as much as possible.

In some cases, network engineers may want to implement custom error handling logic based on specific requirements or network conditions. Ansible's flexibility allows users to write custom error handling routines using Python, which can be invoked when certain errors are encountered. These custom routines can be used to handle device-specific errors, such as invalid configurations or authentication issues, or to integrate with other systems for advanced troubleshooting and recovery. By writing custom error handling logic, network engineers can further enhance the robustness and reliability of their automation workflows.

Error management in Ansible for network tasks is a crucial part of ensuring that automation workflows are resilient, reliable, and capable of handling the unpredictable nature of network environments. By using Ansible's built-in error management features and customizing workflows to address network-specific challenges, network engineers can automate complex tasks while minimizing the impact of errors. Whether through retry logic, conditional task execution, or integrating with monitoring and alerting systems, Ansible's error handling capabilities enable network engineers to create more reliable and efficient network automation processes.

Chapter: Securing Ansible Communications with SSH

In modern network automation, security is paramount. As more and more tasks are automated, the need to ensure that communications between automation tools and network devices are secure becomes even more critical. Ansible, one of the most widely used network automation platforms, relies heavily on secure communication protocols to manage devices. One of the most common and secure ways Ansible communicates with network devices is through Secure Shell (SSH). SSH is a protocol that provides secure, encrypted communication over a network, ensuring that sensitive data, including passwords and configuration details, is protected from unauthorized access during automation tasks. Understanding how to properly secure Ansible communications with SSH is crucial for maintaining a robust and secure network automation environment.

SSH has long been the standard for securely managing network devices and servers. It provides a secure, encrypted channel over an unsecured network, which is essential for protecting the integrity and confidentiality of the data being transferred. When Ansible is used to automate tasks such as configuration changes, updates, or monitoring, SSH ensures that all communications between the Ansible control node and the target devices are encrypted. This encryption prevents malicious actors from intercepting or tampering with sensitive data during transmission. For network engineers, securing Ansible communications through SSH is not just about preventing data breaches, but also about safeguarding the network infrastructure and maintaining the integrity of automated processes.

Ansible communicates with remote devices through SSH by default, using SSH keys or passwords for authentication. SSH keys are the preferred method for securing communications, as they offer a higher level of security compared to traditional password-based authentication. With SSH keys, users generate a key pair: a private key that stays on the control machine and a public key that is placed on the target devices. When Ansible executes tasks on remote devices, it uses the private key to authenticate to the remote device, which checks the corresponding public key stored in its authorized keys file. This authentication method eliminates the need to transmit passwords over the network, making it more secure and less vulnerable to brute-force attacks.

One of the most important steps in securing Ansible communications with SSH is configuring SSH key-based authentication. This involves generating an SSH key pair on the Ansible control node and copying the public key to each of the target devices. This process ensures that only authorized control nodes can connect to the network devices, providing an added layer of security. The private key is securely stored on the control node, and only the corresponding public key can be used to authenticate connections to the devices. This method of authentication is much more secure than using passwords, which can be easily intercepted or guessed. Once the key-based authentication is set up, the control node can communicate with the target devices without the need for a password, reducing the risk of unauthorized access.

Another aspect of securing Ansible communications is properly managing SSH key permissions. To ensure that SSH keys are used securely, it is important to restrict access to the private key on the control node. This can be done by setting appropriate file permissions on the private key file, ensuring that only authorized users or processes can access it. Additionally, the SSH public key should only be placed on devices that need to be managed by Ansible, and it should be stored in the appropriate authorized_keys file on the remote devices. By maintaining strict control over the permissions of SSH keys, network engineers can prevent unauthorized access to devices and ensure that the keys cannot be used maliciously if they fall into the wrong hands.

While SSH key-based authentication is the preferred method for securing Ansible communications, it is also important to configure SSH to use strong encryption algorithms and secure ciphers. By default, SSH uses a set of encryption algorithms to secure the communication channel, but these algorithms can be configured to ensure the highest level of security. For example, network engineers can configure SSH to use the more secure RSA or ECDSA algorithms instead of weaker or deprecated ciphers. Additionally, SSH configuration files allow for other security settings, such as disabling root login or enforcing the use of specific key lengths, further strengthening the security of the communication channel.

SSH also supports the use of additional security measures such as two-factor authentication (2FA), which can be implemented to further enhance the security of Ansible communications. While not natively supported in all SSH configurations, integrating 2FA into the SSH login process can significantly increase the security of the connection. With 2FA enabled, users must provide both their private key and a secondary form of authentication, such as a one-time password (OTP) generated by a mobile app or hardware token. This added layer of security makes it much more difficult for attackers to gain unauthorized access, even if they manage to obtain a user's private key.

To further secure Ansible communications, it is essential to configure and maintain firewalls to limit access to SSH services on network devices. By restricting SSH access to only trusted IP addresses and ranges, network engineers can reduce the attack surface and prevent unauthorized systems from attempting to access network devices through SSH. This can be achieved by configuring firewalls on the network devices themselves, as well as on intermediate devices such as routers and firewalls that sit between the control node and the target devices. Additionally, restricting SSH access based on IP address ranges helps prevent unauthorized access from systems that may be outside the trusted network.

Monitoring SSH connections is also a key element in securing Ansible communications. By enabling logging and auditing features on the SSH service, network engineers can track all incoming SSH connections and detect any suspicious or unauthorized access attempts. This includes monitoring failed login attempts, unusual connection patterns, or attempts to use outdated or weak encryption algorithms. SSH logs can provide valuable information for forensic investigations if a security incident occurs, and they can also help identify and mitigate potential vulnerabilities before they are exploited.

In addition to securing the SSH connection itself, it is important to secure the underlying systems running Ansible. This includes keeping both the control node and the target devices up to date with the latest security patches, ensuring that any known vulnerabilities are addressed promptly. Ansible can be integrated with configuration management tools to ensure that devices are consistently configured with the latest security settings, including secure SSH configurations. By implementing regular security checks, applying patches as needed, and monitoring the health of the systems involved, network engineers can further enhance the security of Ansible communications and ensure that the network automation process is secure from end to end.

The use of SSH in securing Ansible communications is essential for protecting sensitive data, ensuring authentication, and preventing unauthorized access to network devices. By implementing SSH key-based authentication, configuring strong encryption settings, managing key permissions, and employing additional security measures like two-factor authentication, network engineers can significantly improve the security of their automation workflows. Monitoring SSH connections, securing underlying systems, and maintaining proper firewall configurations further enhance the security of Ansible communications. With these best practices in place, network engineers can confidently automate network management tasks, knowing that their communications are protected from unauthorized access and potential attacks.

Chapter: Using NETCONF to Retrieve Configuration Data

NETCONF, or Network Configuration Protocol, is a widely used protocol for managing and configuring network devices in an automated and structured manner. It provides a standardized, secure method for retrieving configuration data and operational information from network devices such as routers, switches, firewalls, and load balancers. NETCONF allows network engineers to interact with devices in a consistent way, regardless of the vendor, and retrieve detailed configuration data that is crucial for monitoring and managing the health of the network. Using NETCONF to retrieve configuration data not only simplifies network management but also enhances the visibility and control over network devices.

The core advantage of NETCONF lies in its ability to provide a standardized, XML-based interface for interacting with network devices. Configuration data, which traditionally required manual intervention through command-line interfaces (CLI), can now be retrieved programmatically and automatically using NETCONF. The protocol allows users to interact with devices in a consistent manner, retrieving the running configuration or operational data without having to log into each device individually. This ability to retrieve configuration data from multiple devices at once is especially valuable in large, dynamic networks where manual checking of each device can be error-prone and time-consuming.

NETCONF retrieves configuration data using a set of core operations, one of which is the get-config operation. This operation allows users to retrieve the current configuration of a device or a specific portion of its configuration. For example, network engineers can retrieve the configuration for interfaces, routing protocols, security policies, or other network settings. The get-config operation allows users to specify the exact portion of the configuration they are interested in, providing flexibility and enabling users to gather only the relevant data.

The retrieved configuration data is typically returned in XML format, which is highly structured and easily parsed by automation tools. XML is well-suited for configuration data because it allows for a hierarchical structure that can represent complex relationships between configuration elements. For instance, a configuration file retrieved via NETCONF may contain nested elements that define an interface's IP address, subnet mask, and other properties. XML provides a way to represent this data in a readable format that can be easily processed by network automation systems, allowing for further analysis, modification, or validation.

An important feature of NETCONF when retrieving configuration data is the ability to filter the data using XPath queries. XPath is a powerful query language used to navigate through XML documents, enabling users to extract specific pieces of information from a configuration file. For example, network engineers may want to retrieve only the configuration of certain interfaces or routing policies while excluding other parts of the configuration. By using XPath queries, NETCONF enables users to retrieve only the data that is relevant to their task, improving efficiency and reducing the amount of unnecessary data being transferred.

When using NETCONF to retrieve configuration data, it is often essential to integrate it with network automation tools such as Ansible. Ansible, for example, includes modules that interact with NETCONF-enabled devices, allowing network engineers to automate the retrieval of configuration data. By using Ansible's netconf module, users can easily connect to network devices and retrieve configuration data through NETCONF operations. These tools can automate the retrieval of configuration data across hundreds or thousands of devices, enabling network engineers to gather the latest configurations from the entire network without manual intervention. Once the configuration data is retrieved, Ansible can process it further, such as comparing it with the desired configuration state, checking for compliance, or storing it in a central repository.

One of the key benefits of using NETCONF to retrieve configuration data is the ability to access both running configurations and candidate configurations. The running configuration represents the current operational state of a device, while the candidate configuration is a configuration that has been modified but not yet committed to the device. In certain use cases, it may be necessary to retrieve the candidate configuration to review planned changes before they are committed. NETCONF provides a way to retrieve both types of configurations, allowing for greater flexibility when managing network devices. By retrieving the candidate configuration, engineers can preview changes and ensure that the network is configured as expected before applying the changes to the device.

Additionally, NETCONF supports the ability to retrieve operational data, such as interface status, device health, and resource utilization. This operational data is essential for network monitoring and troubleshooting, as it provides real-time insights into the performance of devices. Using NETCONF, network engineers can retrieve data such as interface statistics, routing tables, or device logs, which can help diagnose network issues, track performance, and ensure that devices are functioning optimally. This data can be integrated into broader network monitoring systems, enabling proactive management of the network and faster resolution of issues.

Retrieving configuration data with NETCONF is also highly beneficial for compliance and auditing purposes. In regulated environments or organizations with strict configuration standards, it is crucial to ensure that all devices are configured correctly and in alignment with organizational policies. By using NETCONF to automate the retrieval of configuration data, network engineers can regularly check the configurations of devices against established standards, flagging any deviations or misconfigurations. This automated process helps ensure that the network remains compliant and that any potential issues are identified and addressed in a timely manner.

Another important aspect of using NETCONF to retrieve configuration data is the ability to compare configurations over time. Configuration drift, which occurs when the configurations of devices change unintentionally, is a common issue in large networks. By regularly retrieving configuration data using NETCONF, network engineers can track changes in device configurations and identify any discrepancies between the current and previous configurations. This helps ensure that configurations are consistent across devices and that any unauthorized changes are detected. NETCONF also allows for versioning of configuration data, enabling network engineers to maintain a historical record of changes and revert to previous configurations if necessary.

Using NETCONF to retrieve configuration data also simplifies the process of backing up device configurations. Regular backups are essential for disaster recovery and minimizing downtime in the event of a failure. By automating the retrieval of configuration data using NETCONF, network engineers can ensure that device configurations are backed up consistently and securely. These backups can be stored in centralized repositories, where they can be accessed and restored if needed. With NETCONF's ability to retrieve detailed and structured configuration data, network engineers can quickly restore devices to their previous state after a failure, reducing downtime and ensuring business continuity.

The ability to retrieve configuration data using NETCONF provides network engineers with enhanced control, flexibility, and visibility over their network devices. By integrating NETCONF with network automation tools like Ansible, engineers can automate the process of retrieving configuration data across the entire network, ensuring that configurations are consistent, compliant, and up to date. Whether used for monitoring, backup, compliance, or troubleshooting, NETCONF offers a powerful, standardized method for retrieving configuration data from network devices. This capability streamlines network management, improves operational efficiency, and helps maintain the stability and security of the network.

Chapter: Structuring Network Automation Projects in Ansible

When implementing network automation, one of the first critical steps is organizing and structuring the project in a way that promotes scalability, maintainability, and flexibility. Ansible, a leading automation platform, provides a powerful framework for managing network configurations, monitoring devices, and automating tasks across diverse network environments. However, as network infrastructures become larger and more complex, it is essential to structure Ansible projects in a way that allows them to scale efficiently while ensuring that automation tasks are well-organized and easy to maintain. This requires not only understanding the core concepts of Ansible but also applying best practices for structuring playbooks, inventories, roles, and variables in a way that suits the needs of a network automation environment.

The first key component of structuring an Ansible project is the use of inventories. Ansible uses an inventory file to define which devices it will manage, as well as to group those devices based on common attributes. In a network automation environment, the inventory serves as the foundation for automation, as it tells Ansible where to connect and what devices to manage. The inventory file can be static or dynamic. Static inventories are simple text files listing the IP addresses or hostnames of network devices, along with any variables or parameters that might be needed for authentication or configuration. Dynamic inventories, on the other hand, allow for more flexibility by dynamically pulling device information from external sources, such as cloud platforms or network management tools. By using a dynamic inventory, network engineers can easily manage devices that are frequently added or removed from the network without having to manually update the inventory file.

Once the inventory is set up, the next crucial aspect of structuring a network automation project in Ansible is organizing playbooks. Playbooks are the heart of Ansible's automation process, containing the tasks and configurations that will be applied to the network devices. When structuring playbooks, it is important to design them in a way that they are modular, reusable, and easy to maintain. One of the best practices for organizing playbooks is to break them into smaller, task-specific files. Each playbook should focus on a single objective, such as configuring interfaces, applying security policies, or managing routing protocols. By keeping playbooks focused on specific tasks, engineers can ensure that they are easy to understand and troubleshoot. Additionally, modular playbooks are easier to reuse, as they can be combined and executed in various configurations depending on the needs of the network.

Ansible allows for the use of roles, which are another important tool for organizing network automation projects. Roles in Ansible are collections of tasks, variables, templates, and files that can be reused across multiple playbooks. Roles help to structure a project in a more organized and logical way, making it easier to manage large-scale networks. For example, a role could be created to configure VLANs on switches, while another role could focus on setting up OSPF on routers. By organizing playbooks into roles, network engineers can easily share and reuse configurations, ensuring that best practices are consistently applied across the network. Roles also allow for better separation of concerns, as each role can be dedicated to a specific network device or function, reducing the complexity of individual playbooks.

Variables play a critical role in network automation, especially when managing devices with different configurations or settings. Ansible allows for the use of variables in playbooks, which helps make the automation process more dynamic and adaptable. When structuring network automation projects, it is important to consider where to define variables to ensure they are accessible and easily maintainable. Variables can be defined in a variety of places, including the playbook itself, in separate variable files, or directly in the inventory file. It is a best practice to store variables that are specific to devices or groups of devices in the inventory file or in group-specific variable files. This helps to keep playbooks more general and reusable, as the same playbook can be used across multiple devices with different configurations simply by changing the variable values.

In larger network automation projects, it is also important to implement proper error handling and logging. Ansible provides several mechanisms for error management, such as using the ignore_errors directive to allow tasks to fail without stopping the entire playbook. This is especially useful in network automation, where temporary connectivity issues or device unavailability may cause certain tasks to fail. Network engineers can structure their playbooks to include error handling mechanisms, such as retries or conditional logic, to ensure that automation workflows continue smoothly even when minor issues occur. Logging is another crucial aspect of network automation, as it provides visibility into the execution of tasks and helps with troubleshooting. Ansible can be configured to generate detailed logs of playbook execution, which can be useful for identifying and addressing issues that arise during automation.

Another important consideration when structuring network automation projects is ensuring that the tasks are idempotent. Idempotency refers to the ability of an automation task to be safely repeated without changing the outcome if it has already been applied. In network automation, idempotency ensures that configurations are applied consistently, even if the playbook is run multiple times. This is critical in environments where network configurations may change frequently, and the ability to reapply configurations without disrupting service is essential. By designing playbooks with idempotency in mind, network engineers can ensure that automation tasks can be safely executed repeatedly, reducing the risk of configuration drift or inconsistencies across the network.

One of the biggest challenges in structuring network automation projects is managing multi-vendor environments. In many organizations, network infrastructures consist of devices from multiple vendors, each with its own configuration syntax and management interfaces. Ansible provides support for a wide range of network devices through vendor-specific modules, but managing multi-vendor networks requires additional considerations. One best practice is to abstract device-specific configurations by using Ansible roles and templates that can accommodate variations between vendors. By writing generic playbooks that are adaptable to different devices and configurations, network engineers can ensure that their automation workflows work seamlessly across all devices, regardless of the manufacturer.

Finally, testing and validation are essential parts of any network automation project. It is important to structure playbooks and roles in a way that makes it easy to test configurations before they are applied to production devices. This can be achieved by using Ansible's --check mode, which allows users to preview the changes that will be made without actually applying them. Testing playbooks in a staging or lab environment before applying them to production systems ensures that configurations are correct and will not cause unintended disruptions. Additionally, network engineers can implement playbook validation by checking the current state of devices before and after applying configurations to ensure that the desired state is reached.

Organizing network automation projects in Ansible is essential for building scalable, maintainable, and flexible automation workflows. By structuring inventories, playbooks, roles, and variables in a way that promotes reusability, modularity, and clarity, network engineers can ensure that their automation efforts are efficient and easy to maintain. Through proper error handling, logging, idempotency, and testing, network engineers can further enhance the reliability and effectiveness of their automation projects, enabling them to manage large and complex network infrastructures with confidence and efficiency.

Chapter: Managing Network Policies with Ansible

Network policies are essential for controlling the flow of traffic, securing network resources, and ensuring compliance with organizational standards. The traditional manual methods of managing network policies, which often involve logging into each device and configuring individual settings, are time-consuming, error-prone, and difficult to scale. As networks grow more complex, network automation has become a crucial solution for efficiently managing network policies across a large number of devices. Ansible, a powerful automation tool, offers an effective framework for automating the management of network policies, allowing network engineers to define, deploy, and enforce policies consistently across the network. By leveraging Ansible, network engineers can automate the entire process of managing network policies, ensuring that devices are configured according to desired standards, reducing human error, and improving the overall security and reliability of the network.

Managing network policies with Ansible involves creating playbooks that define the desired configurations and state of network devices. These playbooks are written in YAML, a human-readable format that allows network engineers to describe the tasks that need to be executed in a structured way. Ansible modules specific to different vendors, such as Cisco, Juniper, or Arista, allow engineers to automate policy management tasks like configuring access control lists (ACLs), setting up routing policies, defining security rules, and managing Quality of Service (QoS) settings. With Ansible, all these tasks can be automated, ensuring that they are applied consistently and efficiently across the entire network.

One of the primary advantages of using Ansible for network policy management is its ability to automate the configuration of policies across a wide variety of devices. Different network vendors often have their own proprietary ways of managing network policies, which can make it challenging to apply consistent configurations across a multi-vendor network. However, Ansible's extensive library of modules for different vendors allows engineers to write a single set of playbooks that can target devices from multiple vendors. For instance, the ios_config module for Cisco devices or the junos_config module for Juniper devices can be used to configure network policies on different devices using a consistent, high-level syntax. This vendor-agnostic approach simplifies the task of managing network policies in large, diverse environments and ensures that all devices are configured according to the same standards.

Another important feature of managing network policies with Ansible is its ability to ensure that configurations are idempotent. In the context of network policy management, idempotency means that the playbooks can be run multiple times without causing unintended side effects. For example, a network engineer might write an Ansible playbook to configure an access control list (ACL) on a router. If the playbook is run multiple times, Ansible will check whether the ACL is already configured as specified and will only make changes if necessary. This ensures that the policy is applied correctly every time, even if the playbook is executed multiple times due to changes in the network or the automation pipeline. Idempotency helps prevent configuration drift, a situation where policies become inconsistent over time due to manual changes or uncoordinated updates.

Ansible's flexibility also enables the automation of more complex network policies, such as routing protocols and security settings. For example, the ios_eigrp or junos_ospf modules can be used to automate the configuration of routing policies on Cisco or Juniper devices, respectively. These modules allow network engineers to define policies for routing protocols like OSPF, BGP, or EIGRP, ensuring that the routing tables are populated according to the desired configurations. By automating the configuration of routing policies, engineers can ensure that traffic flows efficiently across the network, reduce manual errors, and quickly adapt to changes in network topology.

Network security policies are another area where Ansible excels. Security is a critical aspect of network policy management, and Ansible's ability to automate security-related configurations helps ensure that devices are secured in a consistent and reliable manner. With Ansible, engineers can automate the configuration of firewalls, intrusion prevention systems, and other security devices. For instance, Ansible can be used to automate the configuration of access control lists (ACLs) on routers and switches, ensuring that only authorized traffic is allowed to pass through the network. Similarly, Ansible can automate the setup of VPNs, IPSec tunnels, and firewall rules, ensuring that the network is protected from unauthorized access while still allowing legitimate communication.

Quality of Service (QoS) is another critical aspect of network policy management, especially in environments where bandwidth and network resources need to be prioritized. Ansible can be used to automate the configuration of QoS policies, such as traffic shaping, traffic policing, and priority queuing, across network devices. By automating QoS policies, network engineers can ensure that critical applications and services receive the necessary bandwidth and that the network performs optimally even during times of congestion. Ansible's ability to automate QoS configurations ensures that these policies are applied consistently and can be easily updated as network demands change.

Ansible also simplifies the task of ensuring compliance with network policies. Many organizations have strict standards and guidelines for network configurations, especially in regulated industries such as finance, healthcare, and government. By automating the enforcement of these policies, network engineers can ensure that all devices are compliant with organizational standards and regulatory requirements. For example, Ansible playbooks can be written to check that devices are configured with the correct ACLs, routing protocols, and security settings, and alert administrators when discrepancies are found. By automating compliance checks, organizations can reduce the risk of non-compliance and improve their ability to pass audits and assessments.

Automation also plays a crucial role in managing network policy changes. When network policies need to be updated, Ansible makes it easy to roll out changes across multiple devices simultaneously. For example, if a new security policy needs to be implemented across the entire network, an Ansible playbook can be used to push the updated policy to all affected devices, ensuring that the change is applied consistently and without delay. This ability to manage policy changes at scale is particularly valuable in large networks where manual changes would be inefficient and prone to error. Additionally, Ansible's version control capabilities allow network engineers to track changes to network policies over time, making it easy to revert to previous configurations if necessary.

With the ability to automate network policies using Ansible, organizations can streamline their network management processes, reduce the risk of configuration errors, and ensure that their network remains secure and compliant. Whether it's configuring routing protocols, managing security policies, or applying QoS settings, Ansible enables network engineers to automate the entire process of policy management, improving efficiency and consistency across the network. By leveraging Ansible's flexibility and power, network engineers can create more agile, reliable, and secure networks that can easily adapt to changing requirements and challenges.

Chapter: Network Troubleshooting and Monitoring with Ansible

Network troubleshooting and monitoring are two of the most essential tasks in maintaining a healthy and efficient network. These tasks ensure that issues are quickly identified and resolved, and that the network operates within its optimal parameters. Traditionally, network troubleshooting and monitoring involved manually logging into network devices, running diagnostic commands, and checking configurations. However, with the growing complexity and scale of modern networks, manual methods have become inefficient and prone to human error. Ansible, a powerful automation tool, offers an ideal solution for automating network troubleshooting and monitoring. By leveraging Ansible's automation capabilities, network engineers can ensure continuous monitoring, improve issue resolution times, and streamline network diagnostics across diverse devices and environments.

Ansible's ability to automate network troubleshooting and monitoring begins with its core strength: its modules. Ansible modules, specifically designed for network devices, allow network engineers to interact with devices such as routers, switches, and firewalls in a structured and repeatable manner. Modules like ios_facts for Cisco devices or junos_facts for Juniper devices are used to gather vital information from devices, such as their system status, interface statistics, and configuration details. This information is crucial for network monitoring and troubleshooting, as it enables engineers to gain real-time visibility into the operational state of the network.

One of the key advantages of using Ansible for network monitoring is its ability to automate the collection of device facts. Ansible can be configured to regularly query network devices for their operational status, including interface health, CPU usage, memory usage, routing tables, and logs. By using the gather_facts functionality, engineers can collect a wealth of diagnostic data from devices across the network. This data can be stored in a centralized location or processed for analysis, making it easier to detect performance issues, network congestion, or other anomalies that could affect network performance. Automating the collection of facts also ensures that network engineers have up-to-date information about the state of their devices without having to log into each device manually.

In addition to gathering device facts, Ansible can also be used to perform network troubleshooting tasks automatically. When a network issue arises, time is of the essence in identifying and resolving the problem. Ansible playbooks can be created to automate common troubleshooting tasks such as checking interface status, verifying routing configurations, or testing connectivity between devices. For example, if a network engineer needs to determine why a particular interface is down, an Ansible playbook could automatically check the status of that interface across multiple devices, collect the relevant logs, and even attempt to restart the interface if necessary. This automation speeds up the troubleshooting process, reducing the time it takes to pinpoint the issue and apply a fix.

Ansible's flexibility in handling conditional logic allows for even more sophisticated troubleshooting workflows. By incorporating when statements or custom error-handling logic, network engineers can create playbooks that automatically adjust their behavior based on the results of previous tasks. For example, if a task to retrieve an interface's status fails due to network congestion or device unresponsiveness, the playbook could automatically retry the task, wait for a predefined period, or move to the next troubleshooting step. This intelligent handling of errors ensures that playbooks can adapt to varying conditions and continue working towards resolving network issues, even in the face of intermittent connectivity or device failures.

Monitoring is another area where Ansible excels. Network monitoring is essential for detecting potential issues before they escalate into major problems. Ansible can be used to automate the process of collecting performance data and monitoring the health of network devices. Playbooks can be scheduled to run at regular intervals, querying devices for key metrics such as bandwidth utilization, CPU load, memory usage, and interface errors. This data can then be aggregated, visualized, and used to generate alerts or notifications if predefined thresholds are exceeded. For example, if a router's CPU usage exceeds 90%, Ansible can trigger an alert to notify the network engineer so that action can be taken before the router becomes unresponsive. By automating the monitoring process, network engineers can continuously track the health of the network without needing to manually check each device.

Ansible also supports integration with external monitoring tools, allowing for enhanced monitoring capabilities. By integrating with platforms like Nagios, Zabbix, or Grafana, Ansible can contribute data to these systems, enabling a centralized view of the network's performance. This integration allows engineers to correlate real-time data from Ansible with other monitoring sources, providing a comprehensive picture of network health. Additionally, by integrating Ansible with other tools, network engineers can create automated workflows that respond to monitoring alerts by executing remediation actions. For example, if a network monitoring system detects a spike in latency, Ansible can be triggered to automatically adjust the Quality of Service (QoS) settings on affected devices to alleviate congestion.

In complex network environments, configuration drift is a common issue that can cause devices to operate differently than intended. Ansible can be used to monitor and prevent configuration drift by regularly retrieving and comparing device configurations. By defining a desired state in an Ansible playbook, engineers can automatically verify that devices are configured correctly and consistently. If a device's configuration does not match the desired state, Ansible can alert the network engineer or automatically make the necessary corrections. This ensures that network policies, security settings, and other configurations are applied consistently across the network, reducing the risk of misconfigurations and improving overall network stability.

Ansible's ability to scale makes it particularly effective in large network environments. With thousands of devices across different regions, manually monitoring and troubleshooting each device becomes impractical. By using Ansible to automate network monitoring and troubleshooting, network engineers can scale their efforts to handle larger and more complex networks. Ansible's inventory system allows engineers to target specific groups of devices based on roles, locations, or other criteria, enabling them to run monitoring and troubleshooting tasks on a wide range of devices simultaneously. Whether managing a handful of devices or a sprawling global network, Ansible provides the flexibility to manage network operations at any scale.

Another key benefit of using Ansible for network troubleshooting and monitoring is its ability to integrate with version control systems. By storing playbooks in version control platforms like Git, network engineers can track changes to automation scripts, collaborate with team members, and roll back to previous versions if needed. This makes it easier to maintain an organized and well-documented set of troubleshooting and monitoring tasks, ensuring that configurations and processes are consistent and traceable over time. Additionally, version control provides a safeguard against mistakes or regressions, enabling engineers to quickly revert to a known good configuration or playbook when needed.

Automating network troubleshooting and monitoring with Ansible not only saves time but also improves the reliability and consistency of network operations. By providing real-time insights into network performance, automating routine troubleshooting tasks, and ensuring that devices are consistently monitored, Ansible allows network engineers to manage their networks more effectively. With the ability to scale across large environments, integrate with other monitoring tools, and automate remediation actions, Ansible enhances network management and helps ensure that issues are resolved quickly and efficiently.

Chapter: Automating Software Upgrades on Network Devices

Software upgrades on network devices are a critical aspect of network management, ensuring that devices remain secure, performant, and compliant with the latest standards. Traditionally, performing software upgrades on network devices involved manually logging into each device, checking for available updates, and executing the upgrade process step by step. This method is time-consuming, error-prone, and difficult to scale, especially in large or complex network environments. As networks grow in size and complexity, automation has become an essential tool for managing software upgrades efficiently and reliably. Ansible, a widely used network automation tool, provides a robust framework for automating software upgrades on network devices. By using Ansible to manage software upgrades, network engineers can reduce the time spent on manual tasks, ensure consistency across devices, and minimize the risk of errors that could lead to network downtime.

Automating software upgrades begins with establishing a clear process for managing the upgrade lifecycle. This includes verifying device compatibility with new software versions, ensuring proper backup procedures, and testing the upgrade before deploying it across the network. Ansible provides an excellent platform for automating these tasks, ensuring that the software upgrade process is streamlined and repeatable. The first step in automating software upgrades is preparing the network devices and ensuring that they are ready for the upgrade process. This involves checking that the devices meet the necessary requirements for the new software version, such as sufficient memory, available disk space, and proper licensing. Ansible playbooks can be written to check these prerequisites automatically, querying the devices for relevant information, such as available resources and current software versions.

Once the devices are verified and prepared, the next step is to upload the new software image to the devices. Ansible's modules, such as ios_copy for Cisco devices or junos_copy for Juniper devices, allow users to automate the process of copying software images to the appropriate directories on the devices. These modules can be used to upload the software image from a central repository, such as a file server or cloud storage, directly to the target devices. By automating the upload process, network engineers can avoid manual file transfers and ensure that the correct image is uploaded to each device. Additionally, Ansible playbooks can be used to verify the integrity of the uploaded image, ensuring that the file was transferred successfully and is not corrupted.

The next step in the upgrade process is to execute the upgrade itself, which typically involves rebooting the device and applying the new software image. Ansible can be used to automate the execution of the upgrade by issuing the appropriate commands to the devices. For example, the ios_config module for Cisco devices or the junos_config module for Juniper devices can be used to configure the device to boot from the newly uploaded image and initiate the upgrade process. Ansible playbooks can be written to issue these commands automatically, ensuring that the upgrade is executed consistently across all target devices. Once the upgrade is initiated, Ansible can also be configured to monitor the devices during the reboot process, verifying that the devices successfully boot into the new software image.

A crucial aspect of automating software upgrades is ensuring that proper backup procedures are in place before the upgrade begins. This helps to protect against potential issues that may arise during the upgrade process, such as device failures or configuration corruption. Ansible playbooks can be written to automatically back up the device configurations before initiating the upgrade. By using Ansible modules to retrieve the current configuration data and save it to a central repository, network engineers can ensure that they have a reliable backup that can be restored if necessary. Automating the backup process ensures that network engineers do not forget to perform this crucial step and that the network is protected in case of an upgrade failure.

After the upgrade is complete, it is essential to verify that the devices are functioning correctly and that the new software version is working as expected. Ansible can be used to automate post-upgrade checks by querying the devices for relevant operational data, such as interface statuses, routing table entries, and system resource utilization. Ansible playbooks can include tasks that check these metrics and validate that the device is operating within acceptable parameters. If any issues are detected, the playbook can automatically notify the network engineer, allowing for rapid remediation. Additionally, if the upgrade has caused any issues, the backup configuration that was saved earlier can be restored automatically, minimizing downtime and ensuring that the network can be quickly returned to a stable state.

One of the significant benefits of using Ansible to automate software upgrades is the ability to perform upgrades across large networks in a consistent and efficient manner. In environments with hundreds or thousands of devices, manually upgrading each device is not feasible. Ansible allows network engineers to target groups of devices based on specific criteria, such as device type, location, or role, and apply the upgrade process to all devices in that group. This scalability is particularly valuable in large enterprise networks, data centers, or cloud environments, where upgrading devices manually would be time-consuming and error-prone. By automating the process, network engineers can ensure that the upgrade is applied uniformly across the entire network, reducing the risk of discrepancies between devices and minimizing the chance of configuration drift.

Another advantage of using Ansible for software upgrades is the ability to schedule and orchestrate the upgrade process. Ansible allows playbooks to be scheduled to run at specific times, such as during maintenance windows or off-peak hours, when the impact on network performance will be minimal. This ensures that software upgrades are performed at the most convenient times, reducing the disruption to business operations. Additionally, Ansible can be integrated with monitoring tools to trigger upgrades based on specific events or conditions, such as the release of a critical security patch or the need to address performance issues.

Ansible also provides the ability to test software upgrades in a controlled environment before rolling them out to production devices. By using virtualized or test devices, network engineers can simulate the upgrade process in a lab environment, ensuring that the upgrade will not cause any unexpected issues. Once the upgrade has been validated in the test environment, it can be deployed to production devices with confidence. Ansible's ability to automate the testing and validation process further enhances the reliability of the upgrade process and reduces the risk of downtime or failures during production upgrades.

Automating software upgrades with Ansible not only improves efficiency but also enhances the security and compliance of the network. By automating the upgrade process, network engineers can ensure that devices are consistently updated with the latest security patches and software versions. This reduces the risk of vulnerabilities and ensures that the network is compliant with organizational standards and regulatory requirements. Ansible's ability to automate complex workflows and handle large-scale network upgrades makes it an essential tool for modern network management, enabling network engineers to maintain a secure, reliable, and efficient network infrastructure.

Chapter: Integrating NETCONF with Other Network Management Tools

In the era of complex network environments, managing devices and configurations efficiently is crucial to ensure network stability, security, and optimal performance. One of the most powerful protocols for network management is NETCONF, a standardized network configuration protocol that provides a secure and efficient method for managing network devices. While NETCONF is a robust protocol on its own, its full potential is realized when it is integrated with other network management tools. By integrating NETCONF with complementary tools such as monitoring systems, orchestration platforms, and analytics engines, network engineers can automate workflows, improve operational efficiency, and gain deeper insights into network performance.

NETCONF provides a consistent and secure way to interact with network devices, and when combined with other network management tools, it enhances the overall management capabilities of a network. One of the key advantages of integrating NETCONF with other tools is the ability to automate configuration changes and policy enforcement. Tools like Ansible, Puppet, or Chef allow users to define high-level automation tasks and execute them across multiple devices simultaneously. These tools can interface with NETCONF to retrieve device configurations, push new configurations to devices, and monitor the success or failure of tasks. By using NETCONF in combination with these tools, network engineers can ensure that all devices are configured according to the desired state, eliminating the need for manual intervention and reducing the risk of configuration drift.

For example, Ansible's netconf module provides a seamless interface to interact with NETCONF-enabled devices, allowing engineers to retrieve configuration data, apply changes, and execute tasks such as firmware upgrades or security policy updates. When integrated with an orchestration platform like Ansible, NETCONF allows for the automatic execution of complex workflows that span multiple devices and vendors. This integration enables network engineers to manage large-scale environments more effectively, applying consistent configurations, monitoring device health, and ensuring compliance across the entire network without the need for manual intervention.

Another powerful integration is between NETCONF and network monitoring tools like Nagios, Zabbix, or Prometheus. These tools are designed to collect, analyze, and visualize network performance data, such as bandwidth utilization, packet loss, and latency. By integrating NETCONF with these monitoring systems, network engineers can automatically collect and analyze operational data from network devices, gaining real-time insights into the health of the network. For instance, NETCONF can be used to retrieve system health information, such as CPU and memory utilization, from network devices. This data can then be sent to a monitoring tool, where it can be visualized and used to trigger alerts or automated responses. By combining NETCONF's configuration management capabilities with real-time monitoring data, network engineers can proactively manage and troubleshoot network issues, minimizing downtime and optimizing network performance.

Integration with network analytics platforms also offers significant benefits for improving network management. With the increasing complexity of modern networks, it is essential to leverage advanced analytics to optimize performance and predict potential issues.

NETCONF, combined with data analytics tools, can be used to collect and analyze detailed device and network data, allowing for the identification of trends, anomalies, and potential bottlenecks. By integrating NETCONF with analytics tools, network engineers can gain deeper insights into network behavior, optimize traffic flows, and make informed decisions about capacity planning and resource allocation. This integration enables a more proactive approach to network management, helping to anticipate and address issues before they affect performance.

Network configuration management tools, such as SolarWinds or Cisco Prime, also benefit from integration with NETCONF. These tools are widely used for managing network devices, tracking configurations, and ensuring compliance with organizational policies. By incorporating NETCONF into these tools, network engineers can automate the retrieval and comparison of device configurations across the network. For instance, NETCONF can be used to retrieve the current configuration of a device, which can then be compared against a desired configuration or a compliance baseline. This integration allows for automated compliance checks, ensuring that devices are configured correctly and consistently. If any discrepancies are found, NETCONF can trigger remediation actions, such as rolling back to the correct configuration or alerting network administrators for further investigation.

Furthermore, integrating NETCONF with security tools enhances the security management capabilities of the network. Security tools such as firewalls, intrusion detection systems (IDS), and security information and event management (SIEM) platforms can benefit from the integration of NETCONF, as it allows for the automated retrieval of security configurations and real-time monitoring of security-related data. For example, security policies on network devices, such as access control lists (ACLs), firewall rules, and VPN configurations, can be retrieved using NETCONF and analyzed for potential vulnerabilities or misconfigurations. If any issues are detected, NETCONF can be used to automatically apply corrective actions, such as updating security rules or reconfiguring devices to close security gaps. By automating security policy management with NETCONF, organizations can ensure that their network devices remain compliant with security standards and regulations.

Automation of software upgrades is another area where NETCONF's integration with other tools can significantly enhance network management. Software updates are essential for maintaining device security and performance, but they often require manual intervention and can lead to downtime if not handled correctly. By integrating NETCONF with orchestration tools like Ansible, network engineers can automate the process of upgrading device software, ensuring that devices are updated consistently across the network. NETCONF can be used to check for available software updates, upload new firmware images to devices, and initiate the upgrade process. By automating software upgrades with NETCONF, organizations can reduce the time and effort required to keep their network devices up to date, while also minimizing the risk of human error.

NETCONF's ability to integrate with other network management tools also enables better network troubleshooting and fault management. When an issue arises on the network, it is essential to quickly identify the root cause and take corrective action. NETCONF can be used to gather diagnostic data from network devices, such as interface statistics, logs, and error messages, which can be fed into network troubleshooting tools. These tools can then analyze the data and provide insights into potential causes of network issues. For example, if a device is experiencing high latency, NETCONF can be used to retrieve performance metrics from the device, which can then be analyzed by a monitoring or analytics platform to determine if the issue is related to network congestion, misconfigurations, or hardware failures.

Finally, NETCONF's integration with cloud management platforms further enhances the scalability and flexibility of network management. As organizations increasingly move to hybrid or multi-cloud environments, the ability to manage network devices across both on-premises and cloud-based infrastructures becomes critical. NETCONF can be integrated with cloud orchestration tools to manage network configurations and policies across a diverse range of devices, regardless of whether they are on-premises or in the cloud. This integration allows network engineers to extend their automation and monitoring capabilities to cloud networks, ensuring that cloud resources are properly configured and secured, and enabling seamless management of hybrid networks.

Integrating NETCONF with other network management tools significantly enhances the capabilities of network engineers, enabling them to automate processes, improve monitoring, and gain deeper insights into network performance. By leveraging the full potential of NETCONF in conjunction with orchestration platforms, monitoring systems, analytics tools, security solutions, and cloud management platforms, organizations can streamline their network management workflows, reduce manual intervention, and improve network efficiency, security, and reliability.

Chapter: Real-Time Configuration Changes with NETCONF

In modern network management, the ability to apply real-time configuration changes is essential for maintaining network efficiency, security, and overall performance. Traditionally, network configuration changes involved manual processes that were time-consuming and prone to errors. With the increasing complexity of networks and the growing demand for automation, real-time configuration changes have become a vital part of network operations. NETCONF, the Network Configuration Protocol, provides a secure and standardized method for making real-time configuration changes on network devices. By using NETCONF, network engineers can modify device configurations on the fly, ensuring that changes are applied consistently, securely, and efficiently across the entire network.

NETCONF operates as a client-server protocol that allows network engineers to communicate with network devices in a structured and controlled manner. Unlike traditional CLI-based configurations, where commands are executed one by one, NETCONF works with structured data models, typically represented in XML format, to define configurations. This approach enables a more consistent and scalable way of making configuration changes, particularly in large, complex networks. Through NETCONF, engineers can make configuration changes in real-time, applying updates to multiple devices simultaneously without having to manually access each device. This not only reduces the time required to apply changes but also minimizes the risk of errors that could arise from human intervention.

The process of making real-time configuration changes using NETCONF involves several steps. First, the engineer must establish a secure connection with the network device. NETCONF typically uses secure protocols such as SSH or TLS to encrypt communication between the client and the device, ensuring that sensitive data, including configuration details, is protected from unauthorized access. Once the connection is established, NETCONF allows the engineer to retrieve the current configuration of the device, make necessary changes, and apply those changes without disrupting the operation of the network. This real-time interaction is particularly valuable when network conditions change rapidly, and immediate adjustments are required to maintain network stability or optimize performance.

One of the most significant advantages of NETCONF is its ability to perform configuration changes in a transactional manner. This means that configuration updates can be applied in a way that ensures consistency, even in the event of an error or failure. NETCONF provides mechanisms such as the commit operation, which allows engineers to commit changes after they have been validated, ensuring that only complete and correct configurations are applied. If any issues arise during the change process, NETCONF allows for the rollback of changes, restoring the device to its previous configuration without manual intervention. This transactional approach provides a high level of reliability and safety when applying real-time configuration changes, making it ideal for mission-critical networks where downtime or misconfigurations can have significant consequences.

Another key feature of NETCONF is its ability to work with hierarchical data models, which allows for the definition of complex configurations in a structured and organized way. Network devices often require configurations that involve multiple layers of settings, such as IP addresses, routing protocols, and security policies. NETCONF's use of XML-based data models enables engineers to specify configurations in a way that clearly defines the relationships between different elements, ensuring that changes are applied correctly. This structure is particularly useful when making real-time changes to network devices, as it allows for more granular control over how configurations are modified, reducing the risk of errors that could result from manual configurations.

Real-time configuration changes with NETCONF also allow for better integration with network automation tools such as Ansible, Puppet, or Chef. These tools can be used to automate the process of making configuration changes across multiple devices simultaneously. For example, an Ansible playbook that uses the netconf module can retrieve the current configuration of a network device, apply the desired changes, and validate that the changes have been successfully applied. By using automation tools in conjunction with NETCONF, network engineers can ensure that configuration changes are applied consistently and efficiently across the entire network, regardless of the number of devices involved. This not only reduces the amount of manual work required but also ensures that changes are made according to predefined policies and best practices.

In addition to configuration changes, NETCONF can also be used to retrieve real-time operational data from network devices, such as interface statistics, routing table entries, and device health metrics. This capability is particularly useful when making configuration changes in response to network issues or performance degradation. For example, if a network engineer needs to adjust Quality of Service (QoS) settings to prioritize certain types of traffic, they can use NETCONF to retrieve real-time data on bandwidth utilization and latency, allowing them to make informed decisions about where to apply changes. By combining real-time data retrieval with real-time configuration changes, NETCONF enables a more proactive approach to network management, ensuring that the network operates at peak efficiency.

Real-time configuration changes using NETCONF also enhance network security by allowing for the rapid deployment of security policies and patches. Security vulnerabilities in network devices can have significant consequences, and it is essential to apply security updates as soon as they become available. NETCONF allows network engineers to automate the process of applying security patches, updating access control lists (ACLs), and modifying firewall rules across multiple devices simultaneously. This reduces the time required to deploy security updates and ensures that devices remain compliant with organizational security policies. In addition, NETCONF's ability to validate changes before they are committed ensures that security configurations are applied correctly, minimizing the risk of misconfigurations that could leave the network vulnerable.

Real-time configuration changes with NETCONF are also valuable in maintaining compliance with industry regulations and standards. Many organizations are required to adhere to specific security and operational standards, such as those defined by ISO, NIST, or GDPR. NETCONF can be used to automate the process of applying configurations that align with these standards, ensuring that devices remain compliant at all times. By automating configuration changes and policy enforcement, network engineers can reduce the risk of non-compliance and ensure that the network meets the required standards without having to manually monitor and enforce them.

The scalability of NETCONF also makes it an ideal solution for large, distributed networks. In environments with hundreds or thousands of network devices, making real-time configuration changes manually would be impractical and prone to error. NETCONF's ability to interact with devices remotely and apply changes across multiple devices simultaneously ensures that large-scale networks can be managed efficiently and securely. Additionally, NETCONF's ability to integrate with other network management tools, such as monitoring and analytics platforms, allows for real-time monitoring of configuration changes, ensuring that devices remain in their desired state and are performing optimally.

Real-time configuration changes using NETCONF offer numerous advantages for network management, from enhancing operational efficiency to improving security and compliance. By providing a secure, structured, and transactional approach to configuration management, NETCONF allows network engineers to make changes quickly and safely, ensuring that network devices remain stable and secure. The ability to automate these processes further enhances the benefits of NETCONF, enabling network engineers to manage large, complex networks with ease and confidence. Whether used for troubleshooting, optimization, or policy enforcement, real-time configuration changes with NETCONF are a powerful tool for modern network management.

Chapter: Ansible Variables and Facts for Network Automation

In network automation, flexibility and efficiency are key, and one of the most powerful tools available to network engineers using Ansible is the use of variables and facts. These two concepts are fundamental for creating dynamic, reusable, and scalable playbooks that can be tailored to different network environments and conditions. Variables allow users to define specific data points that can be applied dynamically during the execution of tasks, while facts provide detailed information about network devices, which can be used to make real-time decisions during automation workflows. Understanding and utilizing Ansible variables and facts effectively is essential for anyone seeking to streamline network management, improve consistency, and enhance the scalability of network automation solutions.

Ansible variables are essentially placeholders for data that can be defined by the user or pulled from other sources. Variables can be used to store values such as IP addresses, device credentials, interface names, or any other piece of information that may need to change between different devices or network environments. By defining variables, network engineers can write playbooks that are both reusable and adaptable. For example, instead of hardcoding an IP address into a playbook, an engineer could use a variable to represent that IP address, which can then be assigned different values depending on the device or the environment. This makes the playbook more flexible and allows it to be reused for multiple devices or scenarios without needing to be rewritten each time.

There are several ways to define and manage variables in Ansible, each serving different purposes. Variables can be defined directly within a playbook, in an inventory file, or in separate variable files. Defining variables within a playbook is suitable for scenarios where a small number of variables are required, and the scope is limited to a single playbook or set of tasks. However, for larger networks or more complex automation workflows, it is often better to store variables in external files or in the inventory file itself. This allows variables to be organized, centralized, and easily managed across multiple playbooks. Ansible also supports the use of environment variables and can pull data from external systems or APIs, further enhancing the flexibility of variable management.

Ansible provides a powerful set of tools for working with variables, including the ability to create complex variable structures such as dictionaries or lists. For example, a dictionary can be used to store multiple related values under a single key, such as a device's name, IP address, and management credentials. This makes it easier to manage related sets of data and ensures that configurations are applied consistently. Additionally, Ansible supports variable precedence, which determines how variable values are assigned when there are multiple sources. This gives network engineers fine-grained control over which variables take priority in different situations.

Facts, on the other hand, are pieces of information gathered from the network devices during the execution of an Ansible playbook. Facts are automatically collected by Ansible when the gather_facts directive is used, and they provide a detailed snapshot of the device's state, configuration, and performance. Facts include information such as the device's operating system version, available interfaces, memory usage, CPU utilization, and network settings. This information is essential for making informed decisions during network automation tasks and for adapting playbooks to the real-time conditions of the network.

Facts play a crucial role in making Ansible playbooks dynamic and responsive. For example, a network engineer could write a playbook to configure routing protocols, but the specific settings for the routing protocol might depend on the device's model or its current configuration. By gathering facts about the device before applying any changes, Ansible can adjust the playbook's behavior to suit the specific requirements of each device. If the playbook detects that a device is running a particular operating system or version, it can automatically apply the correct configuration commands for that system, ensuring that the task is executed correctly.

Facts are particularly useful for troubleshooting and monitoring network devices. With the help of Ansible facts, network engineers can quickly retrieve real-time data about the status and health of devices. For instance, facts can provide insights into interface status, routing table entries, and the operational state of network devices. This real-time information can be used to make dynamic decisions, such as rerouting traffic or adjusting policies based on the current state of the network. Additionally, facts can be used to verify that configuration changes have been successfully applied, making it easier to ensure that the network is operating as expected.

One of the key advantages of using facts in network automation is the ability to handle varying conditions across devices. Networks are rarely homogeneous, and devices from different vendors or models may have different configurations, capabilities, and performance characteristics. By collecting facts from each device, Ansible can dynamically adjust its behavior to accommodate these differences. For example, a playbook may need to apply different configurations based on the device's hardware capabilities or the specific version of the operating system it is running. With facts, Ansible can automatically determine which configurations are applicable and ensure that the correct tasks are executed based on the device's unique characteristics.

Another important feature of Ansible facts is the ability to filter and customize the data that is collected. Ansible allows users to gather only the specific facts they need for a given task, reducing unnecessary data collection and improving the efficiency of the automation process. This can be particularly useful in large networks where gathering extensive amounts of data from all devices could lead to performance issues or excessive load on the network. By using the gather_facts directive selectively, network engineers can tailor the information that is collected, ensuring that only the most relevant facts are retrieved for each task.

The combination of variables and facts provides a powerful toolkit for automating complex network configurations and operations. By using variables, network engineers can create flexible, reusable playbooks that can be applied across a variety of devices and network environments. Facts, on the other hand, allow Ansible to adapt to the specific conditions of each device, ensuring that configurations are applied correctly and that network performance is optimized. Together, variables and facts allow for more efficient and effective network automation, reducing the need for manual intervention and ensuring that the network remains secure, reliable, and performant.

In addition to simplifying automation, the use of variables and facts helps improve the scalability of network automation efforts. As networks continue to grow in size and complexity, manually configuring devices becomes increasingly impractical. By leveraging variables and facts, network engineers can create playbooks that automatically adjust to different devices, reducing the complexity of managing large-scale networks. This scalability ensures that network automation can keep pace with the growing demands of modern networks, providing a consistent and reliable approach to managing configurations, monitoring performance, and troubleshooting issues across a wide range of devices and environments.

Ansible's variables and facts are fundamental to the success of network automation efforts. By enabling dynamic, adaptable playbooks and automating the process of gathering and using device-specific information, these features ensure that network automation tasks are efficient, reliable, and scalable. As the role of automation continues to expand in network management, understanding how to effectively use variables and facts will be essential for optimizing the performance, security, and reliability of network infrastructures.

Chapter: Writing Complex Playbooks for Multi-Device Management

In modern network management, managing configurations and tasks across a wide variety of devices is a critical requirement. With an increasing number of devices and manufacturers in the network, network engineers must find efficient ways to apply configurations and ensure that devices are in sync. Ansible, a powerful automation tool, is particularly useful in these scenarios due to its ability to automate tasks across multiple devices, making network management more streamlined and consistent. Writing complex playbooks for multi-device management involves a combination of understanding the network topology, utilizing Ansible's extensive modules, and leveraging the platform's ability to handle multiple devices in parallel. Through well-structured playbooks, network engineers can ensure that tasks like configuration updates, security patching, and policy enforcement are executed seamlessly across an entire network.

Ansible playbooks provide a flexible and repeatable framework for automating tasks on multiple devices. In a multi-device environment, one of the first steps in writing complex playbooks is organizing the inventory. Ansible's inventory system allows devices to be grouped based on various criteria such as device role, location, or manufacturer. This makes it possible to define specific variables and configurations for each group, allowing network engineers to target different types of devices without having to modify the playbook. For example, you could have one group for routers, another for switches, and a third for firewalls. Each of these groups can have different configurations or tasks applied to them, but they can all be managed through the same playbook. By organizing the devices in this way, Ansible can apply specific configurations to each device type, ensuring that each device receives the correct settings based on its role.

When writing complex playbooks, one of the key features to leverage is Ansible's ability to handle multiple devices simultaneously. Instead of having to write separate playbooks for each device or device group, engineers can create playbooks that execute tasks on all devices in parallel. This is particularly useful for tasks that need to be applied consistently across the entire network, such as software upgrades, security patches, or configuration changes. For example, a playbook could be written to update the firmware on all routers and switches simultaneously, ensuring that the network is updated in a single operation without the need for separate tasks for each device. By taking advantage of parallel execution, Ansible allows for significant time savings and ensures that configurations are applied uniformly across devices.

Another powerful feature of Ansible when working with multiple devices is the use of conditionals and loops. These constructs allow engineers to write more dynamic playbooks that can adjust based on the device's status, role, or configuration. For example, a conditional might be used to check whether a device is running a specific version of an operating system before applying a configuration change. If the device is already running the desired version, the playbook could skip that task and move on to the next. Similarly, loops can be used to apply a configuration across multiple devices or interfaces, reducing redundancy and ensuring that tasks are applied uniformly. This is especially useful when configuring network devices like switches, where the same set of configurations may need to be applied to multiple interfaces.

Variables play a significant role in writing complex playbooks for multi-device management. Using variables, network engineers can make playbooks more flexible and reusable across different devices and environments. Ansible allows for variables to be defined at multiple levels: globally within the playbook, in inventory files, or in external variable files. Variables can also be dynamic, meaning that they can be pulled from other systems or retrieved from the devices themselves using Ansible's fact-gathering capabilities. For example, a variable could be used to define an interface's IP address, allowing the playbook to automatically apply the correct IP address to the appropriate interface across all devices. Using variables in this way allows for the creation of playbooks that can be used in various contexts without modification, significantly improving scalability and reducing the need for repetitive tasks.

Handling errors and ensuring that the playbook executes successfully across multiple devices is another key consideration when writing complex playbooks. In multi-device environments, it's inevitable that some tasks will fail due to connectivity issues, device-specific configurations, or other factors. Ansible provides several tools for managing errors, such as the ignore_errors directive, which allows the playbook to continue execution even when a task fails. Additionally, the retries and delay options can be used to automatically retry tasks in case of temporary failures, ensuring that tasks have multiple opportunities to succeed before the playbook moves on. It is also possible to define custom error-handling routines, which can notify administrators or trigger remediation actions when certain tasks fail. These mechanisms ensure that playbooks are resilient and capable of handling common errors that may arise during multi-device operations.

Logging and tracking the execution of playbooks is an essential part of managing multi-device environments. With large-scale automation, it's critical to maintain visibility into the success or failure of tasks, particularly when tasks are being executed across a large number of devices. Ansible provides detailed logging options that allow engineers to monitor the progress of the playbook and troubleshoot issues when they arise. Logs can include information about each task's execution status, any errors encountered, and the output of commands run on the devices. By reviewing these logs, network engineers can gain valuable insights into the behavior of the playbook and take corrective action when necessary. Additionally, Ansible's integration with monitoring systems can trigger alerts or notifications based on playbook outcomes, further enhancing the visibility of network automation processes.

Security is another critical consideration when writing complex playbooks for multi-device management. Network devices often store sensitive information, such as passwords, configurations, and security policies, making it essential to protect this data during automation tasks. Ansible provides several security features to ensure that sensitive data is encrypted and handled securely. For example, Ansible Vault can be used to encrypt sensitive variables, such as passwords, ensuring that they are not stored in plain text in playbooks or variable files. Additionally, when working with network devices, engineers can use secure communication methods such as SSH or TLS to encrypt the data being transmitted between Ansible and the devices. By leveraging these security features, network engineers can ensure that their automation workflows are secure and compliant with organizational policies.

The scalability of Ansible is one of its most powerful features, particularly when working with multi-device environments. As networks grow in size and complexity, managing configurations and tasks manually becomes increasingly difficult. By writing complex playbooks that automate the configuration and management of large numbers of devices, network engineers can maintain control over even the most extensive networks. Ansible's flexibility allows engineers to handle networks of any size, from small branch offices to large data centers or global infrastructures. The ability to target groups of devices, execute tasks in parallel, and use variables to adapt to different devices makes Ansible an ideal solution for managing multi-device networks.

Writing complex playbooks for multi-device management is an essential skill for network engineers seeking to streamline network operations, ensure consistency across devices, and improve efficiency. By organizing devices into inventory groups, using conditionals and loops, leveraging variables, and handling errors effectively, engineers can create playbooks that automate even the most complex network tasks. The ability to securely manage large-scale networks, monitor progress, and maintain visibility into playbook execution ensures that network automation can scale efficiently as the network grows. With Ansible, network engineers can manage large, dynamic, multi-device environments with confidence and ease.

Chapter: Best Practices for Network Automation with Ansible

Network automation has become a critical aspect of modern network management, offering significant improvements in efficiency, consistency, and scalability. With Ansible, network engineers can automate a wide variety of tasks, such as configuring devices, applying security policies, monitoring performance, and deploying updates. However, to fully leverage the power of Ansible in network automation, it is essential to follow best practices that ensure the automation process is efficient, secure, and reliable. Implementing these best practices helps avoid common pitfalls, reduces the risk of errors, and enables smoother network management workflows across diverse network environments.

One of the foundational best practices for network automation with Ansible is the effective organization of inventory files. Inventory files define the devices and groups of devices that Ansible will manage. Organizing the inventory in a structured way is crucial, especially in large or complex networks. Devices should be grouped based on roles, such as routers, switches, firewalls, and load balancers, or based on geographical location, network segment, or environment (e.g., production, staging, or development). By organizing the inventory effectively, network engineers can target specific groups of devices for particular tasks, ensuring that configurations are applied consistently and appropriately. Furthermore, dynamic inventories can be used to automatically pull device data from external systems, such as cloud platforms or network monitoring tools, making it easier to keep the inventory up to date as the network evolves.

Variables are another critical component of Ansible playbooks, and managing them effectively is key to building maintainable and flexible network automation workflows. Instead of hardcoding values, such as IP addresses or device credentials, into playbooks, variables should be used to represent these values. This allows playbooks to be reused across different environments and devices without modification. Ansible allows variables to be defined at multiple levels, including in playbooks, inventory files, or external variable files. The use of variables also helps avoid errors that can occur when hardcoding values, such as mismatches between devices or environments. It is also important to keep variables organized and to use clear naming conventions to ensure that the playbooks remain easy to understand and maintain over time.

Another best practice is to ensure that Ansible playbooks are idempotent. Idempotency refers to the property where running the same playbook multiple times does not change the outcome after the first execution. This is crucial in network automation because network configurations should remain consistent, even if a playbook is executed more than once. When designing playbooks, network engineers should ensure that tasks are written in a way that prevents unnecessary changes. For example, when configuring an interface on a router, a playbook should check the current configuration first and only apply the changes if they are necessary. This prevents the network from being unnecessarily altered, reduces the risk of errors, and ensures that devices are not inadvertently reconfigured.

Effective error handling is another best practice that should be incorporated into Ansible playbooks for network automation. Network automation workflows are often executed in complex environments where network issues, device failures, or misconfigurations can lead to errors. To ensure that playbooks can handle these situations gracefully, engineers should implement error-handling mechanisms, such as retries, conditional logic, and custom error messages. For example, if a playbook encounters a timeout or connection failure while attempting to configure a device, it can automatically retry the task a specified number of times before moving on to the next task. This ensures that temporary network issues do not disrupt the overall automation process. Additionally, custom error messages and logging should be used to provide clear feedback about issues, making it easier for engineers to diagnose and resolve problems.

Security is always a primary concern when automating network management, particularly when sensitive information, such as device credentials or security configurations, is involved. To mitigate security risks, best practices should include the use of secure methods for managing and transmitting sensitive data. Ansible Vault is an excellent tool for encrypting sensitive information, such as passwords or API keys, so that they are not stored in plain text in playbooks or variable files. By using Ansible Vault, network engineers can securely manage credentials and other sensitive data while still automating network tasks. Furthermore, when automating network tasks, engineers should ensure that communication between Ansible and network devices is encrypted using secure protocols such as SSH or TLS, preventing unauthorized access and ensuring that sensitive data is protected during transmission.

When managing network devices across multiple vendors, it is essential to ensure that playbooks are vendor-agnostic. Modern networks often consist of devices from multiple vendors, each with its own configuration syntax and requirements. To avoid the complexity of writing separate playbooks for each vendor, engineers should use Ansible's modular approach to interact with devices using common modules and data structures. By abstracting device-specific configurations, engineers can write playbooks that work across devices from different vendors, making the automation process more efficient and scalable. Ansible provides a wide range of modules for various network devices, including Cisco, Juniper, and Arista, allowing engineers to manage devices from multiple vendors using a unified framework.

Testing and validation are also critical aspects of network automation. Before running a playbook on a production network, it should always be tested in a controlled environment, such as a lab or staging network. Testing allows network engineers to verify that the playbook functions as expected and that no unintended changes or disruptions occur. Ansible provides the --check mode, which allows users to preview the changes that would be made by a playbook without actually applying them. This is useful for validating playbooks before execution, ensuring that they produce the desired results. Additionally, once a playbook has been executed, network engineers should validate that the configurations have been applied correctly by gathering facts from the devices and comparing them to the desired state.

To further enhance the effectiveness of network automation, it is important to integrate Ansible with other network management tools, such as monitoring systems, analytics platforms, and ticketing systems. By integrating Ansible with monitoring tools like Nagios, Zabbix, or Prometheus, network engineers can automatically retrieve real-time data from devices, such as CPU utilization, memory usage, and interface status. This data can then be used to trigger automation tasks, such as adjusting QoS settings or applying configuration changes in response to network issues. Additionally, integrating Ansible with ticketing systems like Jira or ServiceNow can streamline incident management by automatically creating tickets when issues are detected, allowing engineers to track and resolve problems more efficiently.

Documentation is an often-overlooked but crucial best practice in network automation. Well-documented playbooks, variables, and inventory files make it easier for other team members to understand, modify, and maintain the automation process. Clear documentation should include detailed explanations of each task in the playbook, the purpose of specific variables, and the overall workflow. This helps ensure that network automation remains maintainable over time, even as network environments change or new engineers take over the automation process.

By following these best practices for network automation with Ansible, network engineers can create robust, scalable, and secure automation workflows that streamline network management tasks, reduce the risk of errors, and ensure consistency across devices. Whether automating routine configuration tasks, applying security policies, or monitoring network health, Ansible provides a powerful framework for modern network management. By incorporating these best practices, engineers can maximize the potential of Ansible and ensure that their network automation efforts are efficient, reliable, and secure.

Chapter: Handling Network Topology Changes Automatically

As networks grow and evolve, topology changes become inevitable. These changes can range from adding or removing network devices to modifying network connections, such as switching to a new routing protocol, updating IP address schemes, or reconfiguring VLANs. Such changes, when managed manually, can lead to mistakes, inconsistencies, and network outages. To maintain the efficiency and reliability of a network, it is crucial to automate the process of handling topology changes. Ansible, with its extensive automation capabilities, offers an excellent framework for managing these changes automatically. By leveraging Ansible, network engineers can ensure that topology changes are applied consistently, accurately, and without disruptions to the overall network infrastructure.

Handling network topology changes automatically with Ansible begins with ensuring that the network is mapped correctly. A clear understanding of the existing topology is essential when making any changes, whether it's adding new devices, upgrading hardware, or reconfiguring network paths. Ansible can be used to collect real-time data from devices to create an up-to-date inventory of the network, allowing engineers to identify which devices are affected by changes and need to be reconfigured. By integrating with network discovery tools or using modules like ios_facts or junos_facts, Ansible can pull in configuration data from network devices, ensuring that the automation process is based on the most current topology.

Once the network topology is mapped and understood, automation can be used to implement changes without the risk of misconfigurations. For example, when adding new devices to the network, Ansible playbooks can be written to automate the process of configuring these devices according to predefined policies. These playbooks can include tasks to configure interfaces, assign IP addresses, configure routing protocols, and even apply security policies, all based on the topology of the network. By automating this process, network engineers can ensure that new devices are integrated into the network with minimal manual intervention, reducing the risk of errors and speeding up deployment times.

When dealing with topology changes, particularly those that affect routing and traffic flow, Ansible can be used to automatically reconfigure devices to ensure that they remain aligned with the desired network architecture. For instance, if a new router or switch is added to the network, Ansible can automatically configure the necessary routing protocols, such as OSPF or BGP, across the entire network. By automatically applying the correct configuration, Ansible helps ensure that the new device integrates seamlessly with the existing network infrastructure. This is particularly important in large-scale environments where manual configuration of each device would be impractical and time-consuming.

Similarly, when changes in the network topology require the modification of IP address schemes or VLAN configurations, Ansible can automate the entire process. For example, if the network topology is being restructured, and a new subnet needs to be assigned, Ansible can be used to apply the new IP addresses to the relevant interfaces on network devices. By automating this process, engineers can ensure that the entire network is updated consistently, reducing the likelihood of configuration mismatches or addressing errors. Additionally, Ansible playbooks can include checks to verify that the changes have been applied successfully, providing an added layer of validation to ensure that the network operates as expected after the changes are made.

One of the key benefits of using Ansible to manage topology changes automatically is the ability to maintain consistency across the entire network. Networks are often composed of devices from multiple vendors, each with different configuration syntax and management interfaces. Manually configuring each device can lead to discrepancies, where different devices have slightly different configurations, which can lead to network instability or outages. By using Ansible, engineers can ensure that configurations are applied uniformly across all devices, regardless of the vendor. Ansible's vendor-specific modules, such as ios_config for Cisco devices or junos_config for Juniper devices, abstract the differences between devices and allow network engineers to apply consistent configurations across a multi-vendor environment.

Handling network topology changes automatically also improves network scalability. As networks expand, the number of devices and connections increases, making manual configuration more complex and error-prone. By automating topology changes, network engineers can scale their networks more easily without having to spend excessive amounts of time on configuration. Whether it is adding new switches, routers, firewalls, or even network segments, Ansible allows engineers to automate the configuration process, ensuring that each new addition to the network is configured properly and consistently with the existing topology.

Another benefit of automating network topology changes with Ansible is the ability to quickly respond to network failures or disruptions. In some cases, a topology change might be necessary in response to network issues, such as a failed link, hardware failure, or high levels of congestion. In these situations, Ansible can be used to automatically adjust the network configuration to reroute traffic, reassign IP addresses, or adjust routing protocols to restore network performance. For example, if a critical link fails, Ansible playbooks can automatically detect the failure and trigger rerouting of traffic to alternate paths, minimizing downtime and ensuring the network remains operational. This level of automation helps network engineers quickly adapt to changes in the network and reduces the risk of prolonged outages or service interruptions.

Furthermore, Ansible's ability to integrate with other monitoring and orchestration tools enhances its capability to handle network topology changes automatically. By integrating with tools like Nagios, Zabbix, or Grafana, Ansible can receive real-time alerts about network performance, device status, or topology changes. When an issue is detected, such as a network link failure or device unavailability, Ansible can automatically trigger playbooks to reconfigure the network and address the issue. This tight integration between Ansible and monitoring tools allows for proactive network management, where changes are applied dynamically in response to changing network conditions.

Security considerations are also an important factor when automating topology changes. As network configurations change, it is critical to ensure that security policies and access controls are maintained. Ansible can be used to automatically apply security policies alongside topology changes, ensuring that the network remains secure as it evolves. For example, if new devices are added to the network, Ansible can automatically configure firewall rules, access control lists (ACLs), and VPN settings to ensure that the new devices are secure and compliant with organizational security policies. By integrating security policies directly into the automation workflow, network engineers can ensure that their networks remain secure and protected against unauthorized access, even as the topology evolves.

Handling network topology changes automatically with Ansible provides network engineers with the ability to manage complex, dynamic networks more effectively. By automating the configuration of devices, managing IP address schemes, and ensuring consistency across the network, Ansible reduces the risk of errors and accelerates the deployment of new devices and configurations. It also enhances network scalability and reliability, enabling engineers to quickly adapt to network failures or changes. Through its integration with other tools, Ansible provides a comprehensive solution for managing network topologies automatically, ensuring that networks remain stable, secure, and efficient as they evolve.

Chapter: Developing Custom Ansible Roles for Network Tasks

Ansible is a versatile automation tool that allows network engineers to manage network devices, configure settings, deploy updates, and perform troubleshooting tasks with ease. One of Ansible's most powerful features is its ability to modularize automation tasks through the use of roles. Roles allow for the reusability and organization of playbooks, making it easier to scale and maintain complex network automation tasks. However, out-of-the-box Ansible roles might not cover all the specific requirements of a network environment. This is where developing custom Ansible roles comes into play. Custom roles allow network engineers to tailor automation tasks to the unique needs of their network, making it possible to manage specific network configurations, security policies, and operational workflows more efficiently. By creating custom roles for network tasks, engineers can enhance the flexibility and scalability of their network automation efforts.

A custom Ansible role is essentially a directory structure that organizes tasks, variables, handlers, files, templates, and other resources into a coherent and reusable unit. Developing these roles requires a clear understanding of the tasks to be automated, the devices or systems involved, and the configuration management needs of the network. When creating a custom role for network tasks, the first step is to define the role's purpose. This could be anything from configuring network interfaces on routers and switches, to automating the deployment of security policies, or even managing routing protocols like OSPF or BGP. Understanding the scope of the role helps determine which tasks, variables, templates, and files will be necessary to complete the job.

The heart of an Ansible role lies in its tasks. Tasks define the actions that will be executed on the network devices during the automation process. For example, a custom role for configuring a network switch may contain tasks that configure VLANs, set up port security, and apply QoS settings. Each of these tasks will use specific Ansible modules that correspond to the device's operating system. For Cisco devices, modules like ios_config or ios_interface might be used, while for Juniper devices, modules like junos_config or junos_interface would be more appropriate. Writing custom tasks for network devices involves using these modules to define the desired state of the device and ensuring that the configuration is applied correctly. The tasks must also be idempotent, meaning that they should ensure the desired configuration is applied regardless of whether the task is run multiple times.

Alongside tasks, variables play a crucial role in making custom roles flexible and reusable. Variables in Ansible allow engineers to define dynamic configurations, such as IP addresses, device names, or authentication credentials, that can be applied across multiple devices or environments. For instance, if a network engineer is deploying a role to configure routers, variables might be used to define interface IP addresses, subnet masks, or routing protocol settings. By using variables, engineers can ensure that the same role can be reused across different network devices or environments with minimal modification. Variables can be defined in a variety of places, including the role's main directory, in external variable files, or directly within the playbook. Ensuring that variables are well-organized and clearly defined is critical to making the role easily maintainable and scalable.

In addition to tasks and variables, handlers are an important component of custom roles. Handlers are tasks that are executed only when notified by another task. For example, when a configuration change is made to a network device, the handler might be triggered to restart a service or reload the device. Handlers ensure that actions are only taken when necessary, avoiding unnecessary downtime or performance degradation. For instance, after configuring a routing protocol, a handler might be triggered to restart the protocol process on the device to apply the changes. Developing handlers that are tightly coupled with the tasks in a custom role allows network engineers to maintain a high level of control over the timing of configuration changes, ensuring that devices are configured with minimal disruption.

Another key element in developing custom roles for network tasks is the use of templates. Templates are often used in network automation to manage configuration files or other dynamic content. Ansible uses the Jinja2 templating engine, which allows engineers to create templates that can be populated with variables or dynamic data. For example, a template might be used to generate a configuration file for a router or switch, with specific settings like IP addresses, VLANs, or interface descriptions dynamically populated based on the variables defined in the playbook or role. Using templates in custom roles makes it easier to manage complex configurations, as engineers can create a single template that applies to all devices, with the actual values being filled in at runtime.

Files are also often part of custom roles. Network automation often involves working with static files, such as configuration files or scripts, that need to be copied to devices. Ansible allows engineers to define files that should be copied to the target devices as part of the role. For example, a custom role might involve copying a security configuration file to multiple firewalls in a network. These files can be placed in the role's files directory, and Ansible will automatically handle the copying process. By centralizing files within the role, network engineers can maintain a clean and organized automation environment, ensuring that all necessary resources are easily accessible and correctly applied.

The modular nature of Ansible roles makes them a perfect fit for automating network tasks. Once a custom role has been developed, it can be reused across multiple playbooks or even across different network environments. This modularity significantly reduces redundancy and ensures that network configurations are applied consistently, regardless of the size or complexity of the network. As the network grows and new tasks need to be automated, custom roles can be extended or combined to accommodate the changing requirements. For example, an engineer may start by developing a role for configuring a basic network device, but as the network evolves, the role can be expanded to include more advanced tasks, such as integrating security policies or automating firmware updates.

To ensure that custom roles are reliable and error-free, it is important to test them thoroughly before deployment. Ansible provides tools like ansible-lint to check for syntax errors, and engineers can also use dry-run modes to test roles in a controlled environment before applying them to production devices. Testing custom roles in staging or lab environments ensures that the roles function as expected and reduces the risk of misconfigurations or network outages when the roles are executed in live environments.

As network environments continue to grow and become more complex, custom Ansible roles are becoming an increasingly vital part of network automation. By developing roles that are modular, flexible, and scalable, network engineers can automate complex tasks with greater efficiency and consistency. Custom roles allow engineers to target specific network devices, apply consistent configurations, and ensure that the network is configured according to predefined standards. With proper planning and development, Ansible roles can greatly enhance network automation efforts, improving both the speed and reliability of network operations.

Error Recovery Strategies in Network Automation

Network automation plays an essential role in modern network management, providing a way to efficiently configure, monitor, and manage networks. However, like any complex system, network automation is subject to errors, both during configuration and in the ongoing management process. Ensuring robust error recovery strategies is critical to maintaining operational continuity, especially in large-scale networks where the impact of a failure can be significant. A sound error recovery strategy can not only prevent service disruptions but also minimize downtime and improve the overall reliability of automated systems.

One of the fundamental aspects of network automation error recovery is ensuring that automation processes are resilient to unexpected conditions. Errors can occur due to various factors, including misconfigurations, connectivity issues, or failures in the underlying automation tools. To handle such errors effectively, automation systems must be designed with several key features, such as state validation, logging, and rollback capabilities. State validation is critical because it ensures that the network is in the expected state after an operation is completed. If the state does not align with expectations, corrective actions can be triggered immediately, either by retrying the operation or invoking a predefined recovery process.

The role of logging in error recovery cannot be overstated. Detailed logs provide the insights needed to diagnose issues when they arise and help identify patterns that may indicate recurring problems. Logs can also help in tracing back to the root cause of a failure, allowing network engineers to address the issue with greater precision. Furthermore, comprehensive logging ensures that recovery actions are taken with full awareness of what went wrong, enabling more informed decisions. For instance, if a network device configuration update fails, the logs can reveal whether the failure occurred due to an authentication error, a timeout, or a conflicting setting.

Rollback mechanisms are another cornerstone of effective error recovery strategies. Rollback provides an essential safety net by reverting network configurations to a known good state in the event of a failure. For network automation systems, this often involves using version-controlled configurations and scripts. In the case of an error, the automation tool can automatically revert to the last working configuration, minimizing the impact of the failure. Rollback procedures should be automated and fast, ensuring that recovery happens quickly and without human intervention. A manual rollback process introduces delays and increases the risk of human error, which defeats the purpose of automation in the first place.

To further enhance error recovery, network automation tools should incorporate retry mechanisms. These mechanisms attempt to automatically re-run failed tasks a set number of times before escalating the issue for manual intervention. This approach can be particularly useful in environments where transient issues, such as network latency or temporary service interruptions, are common. Retry logic can help mitigate these types of issues by automatically giving the system another chance to succeed without requiring human oversight each time a failure occurs.

Another crucial element of error recovery in network automation is the ability to isolate problems. In large, complex networks, pinpointing the root cause of an issue can be a daunting task. If an error in one part of the network spreads to others, it can create a cascading effect, causing widespread outages. To minimize such risks, network automation solutions should include mechanisms to isolate problematic components and limit their impact on the rest of the system. By isolating the failure, the system can maintain functionality in other parts of the network, enabling the network team to focus on addressing the specific issue without worrying about further disruptions.

A proactive approach to error recovery includes monitoring and alerting. Continuous monitoring of the network and the automation system provides early detection of issues before they escalate. Automated alerts can notify network administrators of potential problems, allowing them to intervene before the issue affects the entire system. By combining monitoring with intelligent thresholding, automation tools can predict when a task is likely to fail, enabling preemptive actions such as preloading alternative configurations or activating failover mechanisms.

Another layer of protection is ensuring that error recovery strategies align with network design principles. The network should be designed with redundancy in mind, not just for hardware but also for automation paths and management systems. In the event of an error, redundant automation systems can take over the responsibility of task execution, ensuring that operations continue smoothly even when the primary system fails. This approach requires careful planning and a thorough understanding of the network's needs to ensure that redundancy doesn't become a source of complexity or confusion.

In addition to internal mechanisms like state validation and rollback, error recovery in network automation must account for external dependencies. Many network automation workflows depend on external systems, such as authentication servers or third-party APIs. A failure in one of these systems can disrupt the entire automation process. Therefore, it is essential to design error recovery strategies that take external dependencies into account. This could involve implementing fallback procedures that allow the automation system to continue operating, albeit in a reduced capacity, until the external system is restored. For example, if an authentication server is unavailable, the automation system could use cached credentials or switch to an alternative server.

Testing and simulation are vital components of any comprehensive error recovery strategy. Before deploying network automation tools in a production environment, it is critical to thoroughly test them under various failure scenarios. This includes simulating network failures, software crashes, and other common errors to ensure that the automation system behaves as expected during adverse conditions. Simulation allows engineers to fine-tune the recovery mechanisms and ensure that they will work in real-world situations.

Finally, a critical consideration in error recovery is the human element. While automation can handle many aspects of error recovery, there will always be situations where human intervention is necessary. Providing network engineers with the right tools to respond to automation failures is essential. This includes clear communication channels, easy access to logs, and the ability to quickly execute manual commands when needed. By ensuring that automation tools are designed with the needs of the human operators in mind, the system can function smoothly even in the face of unexpected errors.

In summary, error recovery strategies in network automation are essential for ensuring the resilience and reliability of network management systems. Through the use of state validation, rollback, retry mechanisms, isolation of failures, proactive monitoring, redundancy, and consideration of external dependencies, network automation can recover from errors swiftly and efficiently. These strategies enable network administrators to maintain control over network operations, reduce downtime, and minimize the impact of failures.

Using NETCONF for Network Diagnostics

Network diagnostics are essential to ensure the proper functioning of a network, as they help identify, troubleshoot, and resolve issues that may arise within complex network environments. With the growing complexity of modern networks, manual diagnostics can no longer meet the speed and accuracy required for effective management. Network automation tools, such as NETCONF, provide a more efficient approach to managing network devices and conducting diagnostics. NETCONF, a network management protocol, allows network administrators to access, configure, and monitor network devices programmatically. By utilizing NETCONF for network diagnostics, administrators can streamline the process of identifying problems, reduce downtime, and improve overall network performance.

NETCONF, which stands for Network Configuration Protocol, was designed to automate and simplify the configuration of network devices. This protocol works with devices that support YANG data models, providing a structured way to access and manage network configurations. While NETCONF is primarily used for configuration management, it also plays a significant role in network diagnostics. Its ability to retrieve real-time information from network devices makes it a valuable tool for network administrators seeking to monitor the health of their network and troubleshoot issues.

One of the primary benefits of using NETCONF for network diagnostics is its ability to retrieve detailed operational data from devices. This data can be invaluable when diagnosing network issues, as it provides a real-time snapshot of the network's status. With NETCONF, network administrators can gather a wide range of information, including interface statistics, system logs, and device status. This real-time information helps identify anomalies, such as high traffic loads or malfunctioning devices, which may be causing performance degradation or network failures.

In addition to providing real-time operational data, NETCONF supports the retrieval of specific diagnostic information. For example, administrators can query devices for detailed error messages, performance counters, and logs related to specific events. This information is critical for pinpointing the root cause of network issues. Whether the problem is related to hardware failures, misconfigurations, or software bugs, NETCONF allows administrators to extract the necessary data to investigate further. Moreover, the ability to automate diagnostic queries means that administrators can retrieve diagnostic information from multiple devices across the network simultaneously, saving time and improving efficiency.

NETCONF's support for YANG data models is another key advantage when using it for network diagnostics. YANG is a data modeling language that defines the structure of the data exchanged between network devices and management systems. By using YANG models, NETCONF provides a standardized way to retrieve diagnostic information, ensuring consistency across different devices and vendors. This standardization is particularly important in large, multi-vendor networks, where administrators must manage devices from various manufacturers. With YANG, network administrators can create diagnostic queries that work across different platforms, making it easier to collect and analyze diagnostic data from the entire network.

NETCONF's ability to retrieve configuration data also plays a crucial role in diagnostics. Misconfigurations are one of the most common causes of network issues, and being able to quickly compare the current configuration of a device to a known good configuration is essential for troubleshooting. With NETCONF, administrators can retrieve the full configuration of a device, allowing them to identify discrepancies or errors that may be contributing to network problems. By automating the retrieval of configuration data, NETCONF enables administrators to quickly identify and correct misconfigurations, reducing the time spent on manual troubleshooting.

Another important feature of NETCONF for network diagnostics is its ability to perform configuration changes in a controlled manner. When diagnosing a network issue, it is often necessary to make changes to the configuration of a device, such as adjusting interface settings or modifying routing tables. NETCONF allows administrators to make these changes programmatically, ensuring that they are applied consistently across the network. Additionally, NETCONF supports transaction-based operations, which means that changes can be made atomically. This reduces the risk of errors when making configuration changes and ensures that the network remains in a known good state, even if an error occurs during the diagnostic process.

In a large-scale network, it can be challenging to maintain visibility into the status of all devices, especially when dealing with issues that affect only specific segments of the network. NETCONF helps solve this problem by enabling network administrators to retrieve diagnostic information from multiple devices at once. With automation tools that support NETCONF, administrators can query multiple devices simultaneously and collect diagnostic data in real time. This is particularly useful in situations where network issues are intermittent or affect only certain devices. By collecting data from all devices at once, administrators can identify patterns or correlations that may indicate the source of the problem.

NETCONF also facilitates the integration of network diagnostics into broader network management workflows. For example, network monitoring systems can be integrated with NETCONF to automatically retrieve diagnostic data whenever an issue is detected. This allows for a more proactive approach to network management, where diagnostic information is collected and analyzed as soon as a problem is identified, reducing the time to resolution. By automating the process of collecting and analyzing diagnostic data, NETCONF helps ensure that network issues are detected and addressed before they escalate into more serious problems.

The programmability of NETCONF is another advantage in network diagnostics. Using scripting languages like Python or automation tools like Ansible, administrators can write custom diagnostic scripts that collect specific data, analyze it, and generate reports automatically. This level of automation reduces the need for manual intervention and ensures that diagnostic procedures are carried out consistently and efficiently. Custom scripts can be tailored to the specific needs of the network, enabling administrators to perform highly specialized diagnostics based on the unique characteristics of the network infrastructure.

In addition to its core diagnostic capabilities, NETCONF can also be used to integrate with other diagnostic tools and systems. For example, network administrators can use NETCONF to pull diagnostic data from network devices and feed it into other analysis tools, such as network performance monitoring systems or machine learning models designed to detect anomalies. By combining NETCONF's real-time data retrieval capabilities with other diagnostic tools, administrators can gain deeper insights into network performance and identify potential issues before they impact users.

Using NETCONF for network diagnostics also improves the scalability of network management. In large networks with hundreds or thousands of devices, manually retrieving diagnostic data from each device would be time-consuming and error-prone. NETCONF's automation capabilities allow administrators to scale their diagnostic efforts efficiently, ensuring that data from all devices can be collected and analyzed in real time. Whether diagnosing a network-wide issue or a localized problem, NETCONF enables administrators to access the data they need quickly and accurately.

As networks continue to grow in size and complexity, the need for effective and efficient diagnostic tools becomes more important. NETCONF provides a powerful and flexible solution for network diagnostics, offering real-time data retrieval, automation, and integration capabilities. By using NETCONF, network administrators can improve their ability to identify, troubleshoot, and resolve network issues, ultimately enhancing the performance and reliability of their networks.

Automating VLAN Configurations with Ansible

In the modern era of networking, automation has become a cornerstone of efficient management and operation. The ability to automate repetitive tasks can save time, reduce errors, and improve overall network performance. One area where automation is particularly beneficial is in the configuration and management of Virtual Local Area Networks (VLANs). VLANs are used to segment networks into smaller, isolated broadcast domains, which can improve performance and security. However, managing VLANs manually across multiple devices can become cumbersome, especially in large-scale networks. This is where Ansible comes into play, offering a powerful and flexible solution for automating VLAN configurations.

Ansible is an open-source automation platform that enables IT professionals to automate tasks such as configuration management, application deployment, and network provisioning. It uses simple, human-readable YAML syntax for defining tasks, making it accessible to a wide range of users, from network engineers to system administrators. One of the key advantages of Ansible is its agentless architecture, meaning it does not require any special software to be installed on target devices. Instead, Ansible uses SSH or WinRM to communicate with devices, which simplifies the automation process and reduces the overhead of managing agents.

When it comes to automating VLAN configurations, Ansible offers several modules that can interact with network devices, such as Cisco, Juniper, or Arista switches. These modules allow administrators to define VLANs, assign them to ports, and configure other related parameters. By using Ansible, network engineers can create standardized, repeatable VLAN configurations across multiple devices, ensuring consistency and reducing the risk of misconfigurations.

The process of automating VLAN configurations with Ansible typically begins with defining the necessary VLANs in a YAML playbook. A playbook is a file that describes the tasks to be executed, and it is at the heart of Ansible automation. Within the playbook, network engineers can define the VLAN IDs, names, and any other relevant information. For example, a basic VLAN configuration might include defining VLAN 10 as a sales VLAN and VLAN 20 as a marketing VLAN. Ansible's simplicity allows administrators to easily modify these configurations, whether they need to add a new VLAN, modify an existing one, or remove a VLAN from a device.

Once the VLANs are defined, the next step is to assign the VLANs to specific interfaces on network devices. This is an essential part of VLAN configuration, as it determines which devices will be members of each VLAN. Ansible provides network-specific modules, such as ios_vlan for Cisco devices or junos_vlan for Juniper devices, which allow administrators to configure VLAN assignments on interfaces. For instance, if a switch port needs to be assigned to VLAN 10, Ansible can automate this process by defining the port in the playbook and specifying the VLAN membership.

One of the most powerful features of Ansible is its ability to manage configurations across multiple devices simultaneously. In a typical network, multiple switches may be in use, each requiring the same VLAN configuration. Without automation, this would require manually configuring each switch, which is time-consuming and prone to human error. With Ansible, administrators can automate VLAN configurations across all switches in the network with a single command. This not only saves time but also ensures that the VLAN configurations are consistent across the network, reducing the risk of configuration discrepancies.

Ansible also allows for the creation of more advanced VLAN configurations, such as trunking and inter-VLAN routing. Trunking allows multiple VLANs to pass over a single physical link between switches, while inter-VLAN routing enables communication between devices in different VLANs. Both of these configurations are critical in larger networks, where VLANs need to be connected to one another or span multiple switches. Ansible provides modules for configuring trunking on switches, ensuring that the correct VLANs are allowed on trunk ports. Additionally, Ansible can be used to configure routers or Layer 3 switches to perform inter-VLAN routing, allowing devices in different VLANs to communicate with each other.

Another benefit of automating VLAN configurations with Ansible is the ability to implement changes quickly and safely. When a network administrator needs to make a change, such as adding a new VLAN or modifying an existing VLAN, Ansible can apply the changes across the network in a matter of minutes. Moreover, Ansible allows for the use of version-controlled playbooks, which means that changes can be tracked and rolled back if necessary. If a configuration change results in an issue, the administrator can simply revert to the previous version of the playbook and reapply the configuration. This ability to quickly and safely roll back changes ensures that network configurations can be managed with minimal risk.

In addition to the core VLAN configuration tasks, Ansible can be used to automate the monitoring and verification of VLAN configurations. After deploying a new VLAN configuration, it is crucial to verify that the changes have been applied correctly across the network. Ansible provides the ability to retrieve information from network devices, such as VLAN status and interface assignments, allowing administrators to verify that the VLANs are correctly configured and operational. By integrating monitoring into the automation process, network engineers can ensure that any issues with VLAN configurations are detected early and resolved quickly.

One of the key advantages of using Ansible for VLAN configuration is its flexibility. Ansible supports a wide range of network devices from different vendors, making it ideal for multi-vendor environments. Whether a network uses Cisco, Juniper, Arista, or other devices, Ansible can automate VLAN configuration tasks across all devices, regardless of the vendor. This is especially valuable in organizations that have a mix of equipment from different manufacturers, as it provides a single automation platform for managing the entire network.

Ansible also integrates well with other network management tools and systems. For example, it can be used in conjunction with network monitoring tools to automatically adjust VLAN configurations based on network conditions. If a network monitoring system detects congestion or high traffic on a particular VLAN, Ansible can automatically modify the configuration to move traffic to a different VLAN or adjust the VLAN's priority. This integration between automation and monitoring enables a more dynamic and responsive network that can adapt to changing conditions in real time.

Automating VLAN configurations with Ansible is not just about saving time or reducing errors—it also helps improve network consistency and reliability. By defining VLAN configurations in a standardized manner and automating their deployment, network engineers can ensure that configurations are applied consistently across all devices. This reduces the risk of human error and ensures that best practices are followed across the network. Additionally, Ansible's idempotency feature ensures that the desired state of the network is always maintained. If a configuration task is run multiple times, Ansible will make no changes if the network is already in the desired state, further preventing errors and unnecessary changes.

Ultimately, automating VLAN configurations with Ansible enables network administrators to manage complex networks more efficiently. The flexibility, scalability, and ease of use that Ansible offers make it an ideal tool for managing VLAN configurations, whether in small networks or large, multi-site environments. By automating VLAN management, network engineers can ensure that their networks are running smoothly, while also freeing up time for other critical tasks.

Implementing Network Security with Ansible

Network security is a critical aspect of modern IT infrastructure, protecting sensitive data and ensuring the integrity and availability of services. As networks grow in complexity and scale, traditional methods of securing devices and configurations become less effective and more prone to human error. Automation tools like Ansible offer a solution to these challenges by enabling consistent, repeatable, and scalable security configurations across the network. By using Ansible for network security, organizations can enforce best practices, streamline security management, and enhance the overall resilience of their networks.

Ansible is an open-source automation tool that simplifies the management of IT systems by using simple, human-readable YAML syntax. One of its primary advantages is its agentless architecture, which allows it to work with devices that support standard protocols such as SSH or WinRM, without requiring additional software to be installed. This makes Ansible a highly versatile and accessible tool for network security automation. Network engineers can use Ansible to configure security settings on routers, switches, firewalls, and other network devices, ensuring that security policies are applied uniformly across the network.

A key area where Ansible shines in network security is in the configuration of firewalls. Firewalls are the first line of defense in any network, controlling traffic flow based on predefined security policies. Configuring and managing firewalls can be complex, especially in large, distributed environments. With Ansible, network administrators can automate the deployment of firewall rules across multiple devices, ensuring that policies are consistently enforced. By using Ansible modules designed for specific firewall vendors, such as ios_firewall for Cisco devices or junos_security for Juniper devices, administrators can define, apply, and update firewall rules programmatically. This automation not only reduces the risk of misconfigurations but also makes it easier to update firewall policies across the network, ensuring that the security posture remains strong.

In addition to firewall configuration, Ansible is also valuable for managing network access controls. Access control is crucial for preventing unauthorized access to network resources. By using Ansible, administrators can automate the configuration of access control lists (ACLs) on routers and switches. ACLs are used to define which users, devices, or applications are allowed to access specific resources on the network. Ansible allows for the creation and application of ACLs across multiple devices, ensuring that access policies are consistent and up-to-date. For example, Ansible can be used to automate the configuration of ACLs that restrict access to sensitive systems, ensuring that only authorized users or devices can connect to critical services.

Another area where Ansible contributes to network security is in the management of network segmentation. Network segmentation involves dividing a network into smaller, isolated segments to reduce the risk of lateral movement by attackers. VLANs (Virtual Local Area Networks) are a common method of segmenting networks, and Ansible can be used to automate the creation and management of VLANs across network devices. By using Ansible playbooks, network engineers can quickly define new VLANs, assign them to specific ports, and configure routing between VLANs. This ensures that the network is segmented according to security policies, preventing unauthorized access to sensitive areas of the network. Moreover, Ansible can be used to enforce VLAN-based access controls, ensuring that devices in one VLAN cannot access resources in another without proper authorization.

Ansible also plays a significant role in patch management, which is a critical component of network security. Regular patching of network devices is necessary to protect against known vulnerabilities and exploits. However, manually applying patches to network devices can be time-consuming and error-prone, particularly in large environments with many devices. With Ansible, administrators can automate the process of patching network devices, ensuring that updates are applied consistently and on time. By defining playbooks that specify the devices to be patched, the required software versions, and the update procedures, Ansible can automate the entire patch management process. This reduces the risk of devices being left unpatched and vulnerable to attacks.

Compliance with security standards and regulations is another challenge that many organizations face. Standards such as PCI DSS, HIPAA, and GDPR require organizations to implement specific security measures to protect sensitive data. Ansible can help organizations automate the enforcement of security controls required for compliance with these standards. By using Ansible playbooks, network administrators can implement security policies such as encryption, logging, and access controls that align with regulatory requirements. Additionally, Ansible can be used to perform regular audits of network devices to ensure that they remain compliant with security standards. This automation not only saves time but also helps organizations maintain a strong security posture and avoid costly fines associated with non-compliance.

One of the strengths of Ansible in network security is its ability to integrate with other security tools and systems. For example, Ansible can be used in conjunction with vulnerability management tools to automate the deployment of security patches or configurations that address specific vulnerabilities. It can also be integrated with network monitoring systems to respond to security events in real time. When a security event is detected, such as an unauthorized access attempt, Ansible can be triggered to automatically adjust firewall rules, update ACLs, or apply other security measures to mitigate the threat. This level of integration allows organizations to create a more dynamic and responsive security environment.

Automation also helps improve the consistency and reliability of security configurations. In traditional, manual network security management, different administrators may apply security configurations differently, leading to inconsistencies across devices. By using Ansible, security configurations are defined in a standardized, repeatable manner. Playbooks and roles can be reused across the network, ensuring that security policies are consistently applied across all devices. This eliminates human error and ensures that the network security posture remains strong at all times.

Another important advantage of using Ansible for network security is its ability to scale. In large networks, managing security configurations manually can become increasingly difficult as the number of devices grows. Ansible's automation capabilities make it easy to scale security configurations across a large number of devices. Whether an organization is managing a handful of devices or thousands, Ansible can automate the application of security policies across the entire network. This scalability ensures that as the network grows, security management remains efficient and effective.

In addition to its core security features, Ansible's modular design allows for continuous improvements and the addition of new security automation capabilities. As new threats emerge and security best practices evolve, network engineers can easily update and expand Ansible playbooks to address new challenges. The flexibility and extensibility of Ansible make it an ideal tool for maintaining an adaptive, future-proof network security strategy.

Using Ansible for network security automation provides organizations with a powerful tool to enhance the security, efficiency, and scalability of their networks. By automating security tasks such as firewall configuration, access control, patch management, and compliance enforcement, organizations can reduce the risk of human error, improve consistency, and respond more quickly to emerging threats. With its flexibility, scalability, and ease of use, Ansible is an indispensable tool for modern network security management.

Automated IP Addressing and Subnet Management

IP addressing and subnet management are fundamental components of network design and operations. They form the backbone of any IP-based communication, enabling devices within a network to identify and communicate with each other. However, as networks grow in complexity and scale, manually managing IP addresses and subnets becomes increasingly challenging. The need for automation in this area has become more apparent as organizations seek to streamline operations, reduce human error, and improve efficiency. Automated IP addressing and subnet management provide a solution that can simplify these tasks, ensuring that IP addresses are allocated correctly, subnets are optimized for performance, and network administrators can focus on higher-level tasks.

The process of IP addressing involves assigning a unique identifier, known as an IP address, to each device on a network. In IPv4, this address is a 32-bit number typically written in the form of four octets separated by periods, such as 192.168.1.1. Subnetting is the process of dividing a larger IP network into smaller sub-networks or subnets. Each subnet has its own range of IP addresses, and these subnets are used to optimize network performance, improve security, and simplify network management. While these processes are essential, manual IP address allocation and subnetting can be prone to mistakes, especially as the number of devices in a network increases. This is where automation comes in.

Automated IP addressing solutions can streamline the allocation process by using predefined rules and policies to assign IP addresses to devices dynamically. Dynamic Host Configuration Protocol (DHCP) is a common technology used to automate IP address assignment. With DHCP, devices on a network can request an IP address from a DHCP server, which then allocates an available address from a predefined pool. However, while DHCP automates the assignment of IP addresses, subnet management often remains a manual process, requiring network administrators to keep track of IP ranges, subnets, and address usage. This is where automation tools, such as Ansible, come into play, allowing network engineers to automate the entire process, from IP address assignment to subnet management.

Ansible is an open-source automation tool that simplifies the configuration and management of network devices, including routers, switches, and firewalls. With Ansible, network administrators can create playbooks—YAML files that define a series of tasks to be executed on a device. These playbooks can be used to automate tasks such as IP address allocation, subnet creation, and network configuration. By defining rules for IP address assignment and subnet management in Ansible playbooks, administrators can ensure that these processes are executed consistently across the network, reducing the risk of errors and improving efficiency.

One of the key benefits of automating IP addressing with Ansible is the ability to define address pools that are specific to different subnets. Rather than manually tracking available IP addresses and allocating them based on availability, Ansible can automate the process by defining the available address ranges for each subnet. When a new device joins the network, Ansible can automatically allocate an IP address from the appropriate pool, ensuring that addresses are assigned according to the network design. This reduces the administrative burden and minimizes the chances of address conflicts or overlaps.

In addition to automating IP address allocation, Ansible can also be used to manage subnet creation and assignment. Subnetting is a crucial aspect of network design, as it allows for efficient use of IP address space and helps to segment a network into smaller, more manageable sections. By using Ansible, network engineers can define subnets based on specific criteria, such as the number of devices in each subnet, the expected traffic patterns, and security requirements. Ansible can then automatically create subnets, assign them to specific devices, and configure routing to ensure that devices within different subnets can communicate with each other.

Ansible also facilitates the automation of network topology changes. As networks grow, administrators often need to add or modify subnets to accommodate new devices or segments. Rather than manually updating IP address assignments and subnet configurations across multiple devices, Ansible allows administrators to make these changes centrally in the playbook, which can then be automatically applied to all affected devices. This ensures that changes are applied consistently and reduces the risk of misconfigurations that could lead to network outages or performance issues.

In addition to simplifying the management of IP addressing and subnets, Ansible can also be used to monitor and audit network configurations. By automating the collection of network data, administrators can easily track IP address usage, monitor the health of subnets, and identify any potential issues before they escalate. For example, Ansible can be used to periodically check whether a subnet has run out of available IP addresses and automatically expand the address pool if necessary. This proactive approach helps prevent network disruptions caused by exhausted IP address ranges and ensures that the network can scale to meet future demands.

Automation also plays a key role in ensuring compliance with network policies. Many organizations have strict rules regarding IP address allocation and subnetting, particularly when it comes to security and performance considerations. By automating these processes with Ansible, network administrators can enforce these policies consistently across the entire network. For example, Ansible can be used to ensure that certain subnets are reserved for specific types of devices or applications, such as servers or security devices, while other subnets are reserved for general-purpose devices. This helps maintain network integrity and ensures that security policies are applied uniformly across all devices.

Automated IP addressing and subnet management also provide a more efficient way to troubleshoot network issues. When problems arise, network administrators can quickly identify which subnets are affected and determine whether there are any IP address conflicts or configuration errors. By using Ansible to generate reports or alerts, administrators can receive real-time updates on network status, making it easier to diagnose and resolve issues. In large networks, this level of visibility can be crucial for maintaining operational efficiency and ensuring that network performance remains optimal.

The scalability of automated IP addressing and subnet management is another important consideration. As networks grow, the number of devices and subnets can increase dramatically. Manually managing these components becomes increasingly difficult, and the risk of errors rises with the complexity of the network. By automating these processes, organizations can scale their networks efficiently, ensuring that IP addressing and subnet management remains manageable even as the number of devices grows. Ansible's ability to work with a wide range of network devices and vendors makes it an ideal tool for managing large, complex networks with diverse infrastructure.

In addition to simplifying network management, automated IP addressing and subnet management also improve security. By ensuring that IP address assignments and subnets are consistently applied across the network, automation helps to reduce the risk of misconfigurations that could create security vulnerabilities. For example, by automating the segregation of sensitive devices into separate subnets, network engineers can enforce security policies that limit access between subnets and prevent unauthorized communication. Automated management of IP addressing and subnets also makes it easier to audit network configurations and identify any potential security risks.

Automated IP addressing and subnet management are essential for organizations that want to improve network efficiency, reduce human error, and scale their infrastructure. By leveraging tools like Ansible, network administrators can automate the allocation of IP addresses, the creation of subnets, and the configuration of network devices, ensuring that these processes are executed consistently and reliably. As networks continue to grow in complexity, the need for automation in

IP addressing and subnet management will only become more critical, making these practices an essential part of modern network management.

Integrating SNMP with Ansible for Network Monitoring

Simple Network Management Protocol (SNMP) is a widely used protocol in network management and monitoring, enabling administrators to collect and manage data from network devices. It provides a framework for monitoring devices such as routers, switches, servers, and printers by allowing network administrators to query devices for operational data and receive alerts regarding system performance or failures. However, as networks grow more complex, managing and interpreting this vast amount of data manually becomes increasingly challenging. To address these challenges, automation tools such as Ansible can be integrated with SNMP to streamline network monitoring, reduce manual intervention, and improve efficiency.

Ansible is a powerful, open-source automation tool that is commonly used for configuration management, application deployment, and task automation. One of its key features is its ability to integrate with a wide variety of systems, including networking devices that support SNMP. By using Ansible to automate the interaction with SNMP-enabled devices, network engineers can streamline the process of collecting performance metrics, checking device statuses, and responding to network events. This integration allows administrators to automate routine monitoring tasks, freeing up time to focus on more critical network management activities.

SNMP operates through a client-server model, where managed devices (the servers) run SNMP agents, and a management station (the client) sends requests for information to these agents. The information that can be retrieved through SNMP is defined in the Management Information Base (MIB), which is a collection of standardized objects that represent the operational data of a device, such as CPU utilization, memory usage, interface statistics, and more. The SNMP protocol supports both polling, where the management station requests data at regular intervals, and traps, where devices send alerts to the management station when specific conditions occur, such as a link failure or high CPU usage.

Incorporating SNMP into Ansible playbooks allows administrators to automate the process of querying SNMP-enabled devices for specific information. Ansible modules, such as the snmp_facts module, facilitate this integration by allowing users to gather SNMP data from network devices within their playbooks. The snmp_facts module enables the collection of a wide range of SNMP data, including the system's name, description, uptime, and other critical metrics. By embedding SNMP queries within Ansible playbooks, network administrators can automate the retrieval of data, ensuring that it is consistently collected across all devices in the network.

The automation of SNMP data collection provides several benefits. First and foremost, it eliminates the need for manual queries, which can be time-consuming and error-prone, especially in large-scale networks. By automating these tasks, network engineers can quickly access real-time data about network performance, such as bandwidth utilization, packet loss, and error rates, without having to log into each device individually. Additionally, automated SNMP data collection ensures that metrics are consistently retrieved on a schedule, providing a more accurate and up-to-date view of network health.

Ansible's ability to integrate SNMP monitoring into a broader automation workflow further enhances network visibility. For instance, administrators can configure Ansible to automatically run SNMP queries at predefined intervals, ensuring that data is continually collected and analyzed. This automated process can be particularly useful when managing large numbers of devices, as it allows for centralized monitoring from a single playbook, rather than having to manage separate monitoring tools for each device or subnet. By integrating SNMP data collection into Ansible workflows, administrators can create a more cohesive monitoring strategy that spans the entire network.

Moreover, the integration of SNMP and Ansible allows for proactive network management. Network issues often go undetected until they cause service disruptions or significant performance degradation. With Ansible and SNMP, network administrators can automate the collection of critical data points, such as interface status, CPU load, and memory usage, and set thresholds for specific parameters. If a device exceeds a predetermined threshold—for example, if CPU utilization exceeds 90%—Ansible can trigger automated actions, such as sending an alert, initiating a remediation playbook, or adjusting network configurations. This proactive approach enables administrators to detect and address potential issues before they escalate into major problems, improving network reliability and performance.

In addition to automating data collection and proactive monitoring, the integration of SNMP with Ansible enhances network troubleshooting capabilities. When an issue arises, such as a device experiencing high latency or packet loss, administrators can use Ansible to query SNMP data for relevant information that helps pinpoint the root cause of the problem. By gathering SNMP statistics, such as interface error counts or discards, administrators can quickly identify whether the issue is related to hardware, configuration, or traffic patterns. Furthermore, by using Ansible to automate the process of gathering diagnostic data, administrators can quickly collect a comprehensive set of information for analysis, reducing the time required to resolve issues.

Ansible's ability to work with SNMP also facilitates network configuration management. While SNMP is primarily used for monitoring, it can also be employed to configure network devices. By using SNMP write operations, administrators can automate the configuration of certain device settings, such as interface configurations, IP address assignments, or VLAN settings. This capability allows for greater flexibility in managing network devices, enabling administrators to automate both monitoring and configuration tasks from a single platform.

Integrating SNMP with Ansible also simplifies network auditing and compliance. Many organizations are required to adhere to strict regulatory standards, such as HIPAA, PCI-DSS, or GDPR, which mandate certain network security practices and monitoring requirements. By using Ansible to automate the collection of SNMP data, administrators can generate reports that demonstrate compliance with these standards. For example, Ansible can be used to retrieve SNMP data that shows how long devices have been running, the status of critical interfaces, or whether security settings have been applied correctly. This automation makes it easier to generate audit reports, conduct compliance checks, and ensure that the network adheres to necessary security and operational standards.

The integration of SNMP with Ansible also provides a scalable solution for monitoring large networks. In environments with hundreds or thousands of devices, manually querying SNMP data from each device is simply not feasible. Ansible's ability to work at scale enables administrators to query SNMP data from multiple devices simultaneously, reducing the overhead associated with managing large networks. Whether the network consists of a small office with a handful of devices or a global enterprise with thousands of endpoints, Ansible's automation capabilities can scale to meet the demands of any network size.

Ansible's extensive support for SNMP is further enhanced by its ability to integrate with other network management tools. For example, SNMP data collected by Ansible can be fed into a network performance monitoring system for real-time analysis. Alternatively, the data can be used to trigger workflows in other automation platforms, such as incident management or change management systems. This integration allows for a more holistic approach to network management, where SNMP data not only informs daily operations but also feeds into broader IT and business workflows.

By integrating SNMP with Ansible for network monitoring, organizations can enhance their ability to monitor, manage, and troubleshoot network devices. The automation of SNMP data collection and integration with Ansible playbooks enables administrators to gather critical metrics, proactively monitor network performance, and quickly respond to issues. This combination of SNMP and Ansible offers a powerful toolset for maintaining network health, improving reliability, and ensuring that networks are optimized for performance. As networks continue to grow in size and complexity, the integration of SNMP with Ansible will be increasingly essential for efficient and effective network management.

Scaling Ansible Automation for Large Networks

In today's rapidly growing networks, managing devices and configurations manually can become a daunting and error-prone task. With networks becoming more complex and distributed, the need for automation is more critical than ever. Ansible, a powerful and flexible automation tool, can be used to streamline operations, improve efficiency, and reduce human error. However, when scaling Ansible automation for large networks, challenges such as handling a vast number of devices, ensuring performance, and maintaining consistency must be addressed. This chapter explores how to scale Ansible automation effectively for large networks, providing insights into overcoming these challenges and maximizing the benefits of automation.

One of the primary advantages of Ansible is its simplicity and ease of use. It allows network administrators to define tasks in a human-readable format using YAML-based playbooks. These playbooks can automate a wide range of tasks, such as configuration management, software updates, monitoring, and network provisioning. However, as the number of devices increases, so does the complexity of managing these devices. With large networks, executing playbooks against hundreds or even thousands of devices can introduce significant delays and performance issues. Therefore, to effectively scale Ansible automation, several strategies need to be implemented to ensure that tasks are executed efficiently, reliably, and consistently across the entire network.

One of the key challenges when scaling Ansible automation for large networks is managing the inventory of devices. In smaller networks, a simple text file or an ad-hoc list of devices may be sufficient to define the target machines for automation. However, in large networks, keeping track of thousands of devices, including their IP addresses, roles, and configurations, becomes complex. To address this challenge, Ansible provides dynamic inventory capabilities. Dynamic inventory allows administrators to pull the device inventory from external sources, such as cloud providers, configuration management databases (CMDBs), or network management systems. This approach ensures that the inventory is always up to date and reflects any changes in the network. By using dynamic inventory, Ansible can automatically adapt to changes in the network topology, adding or removing devices as necessary without requiring manual updates to inventory files.

Another important consideration for scaling Ansible automation is ensuring that tasks are executed efficiently across large numbers of devices. Running playbooks sequentially across all devices in the inventory can result in long execution times, especially when dealing with complex configurations or large-scale updates. To improve performance, Ansible supports parallel execution, allowing tasks to be executed simultaneously on multiple devices. This parallelism is managed through Ansible's built-in mechanism called "forks," which determines how many tasks can be executed at the same time. By adjusting the number of forks based on the available resources, administrators can optimize the execution time of playbooks. However, while increasing the number of forks can speed up playbook execution, it can also place a strain on the control machine's resources. Therefore, it is essential to strike a balance between parallelism and resource consumption to prevent performance degradation.

In large networks, reliability and fault tolerance become even more critical. A failure during automation tasks, such as a network device becoming unreachable or a timeout occurring during a configuration change, can cause disruptions and lead to inconsistent states across the network. Ansible offers several mechanisms to address these challenges. One of the most effective strategies for improving reliability is to implement retries and timeouts. Playbooks can be configured to automatically retry failed tasks a specified number of times before considering them as failed. This ensures that temporary network issues or device unavailability do not result in playbook failures. Additionally, timeouts can be set for tasks to prevent them from hanging indefinitely, ensuring that playbooks are executed within an acceptable time frame. Another approach to improve reliability is to use Ansible's idempotency feature. Idempotency ensures that playbooks can be safely re-executed without causing unintended changes or errors, even if the playbook has already been applied previously. This is especially important in large networks where playbooks may need to be run multiple times to achieve the desired configuration across all devices.

Another challenge when scaling Ansible automation is maintaining consistency across a large number of devices. As networks expand, the likelihood of configuration drift increases, where different devices may have inconsistent configurations or outdated settings. To mitigate this, Ansible's configuration management capabilities are crucial. By defining network configurations as code in Ansible playbooks, administrators can ensure that configurations are applied consistently across all devices in the network. Playbooks can be written in such a way that they define the desired state of the network, ensuring that devices are configured according to best practices and security guidelines. Additionally, Ansible's role-based architecture allows for reusable configurations, where common tasks and settings can be grouped into roles and shared across multiple devices. This approach ensures that configurations are applied consistently, reducing the risk of errors and improving the overall reliability of the network.

For large networks, organizing and structuring playbooks is essential to maintain clarity, manageability, and scalability. As the network grows, so does the number of tasks and configurations that need to be automated. Without a clear organizational structure, playbooks can quickly become difficult to manage, leading to inefficiencies and errors. One approach to structuring playbooks is by grouping tasks into logical roles based on the function or type of device. For example, separate roles can be defined for routers, switches, firewalls, and access points. Each role can contain tasks that are specific to that device type, ensuring that configurations are applied correctly. Additionally, using inventory groups in Ansible allows administrators to target specific subsets of devices within the inventory, further organizing the automation process. By using this modular approach, playbooks can be easily scaled and extended as the network grows, while ensuring that automation remains efficient and manageable.

One of the most significant benefits of using Ansible in large networks is the ability to integrate it with other tools and systems. In large-scale environments, network management often requires interaction with a variety of monitoring, logging, and orchestration systems. Ansible can be integrated with tools such as network monitoring platforms, configuration management databases (CMDBs), and centralized logging solutions to provide a more comprehensive view of the network's status and health. For example, Ansible can be configured to automatically trigger actions based on monitoring alerts, such as applying configuration changes or adjusting network settings in response to performance issues. This level of integration allows for a more dynamic and responsive network automation environment, where tasks are executed based on real-time data and events.

In addition to integrating with other systems, Ansible can also be used to automate the deployment of network configurations across multiple locations or data centers. In large distributed networks, managing configurations across multiple sites can be a complex and time-consuming task. By using Ansible to automate this process, administrators can ensure that configurations are applied consistently across all sites, reducing the risk of discrepancies and errors. Ansible's ability to manage network configurations at scale ensures that network deployments are efficient and consistent, regardless of the number of locations or devices involved.

Scaling Ansible automation for large networks requires a combination of strategies, including effective inventory management, efficient parallel execution, robust error handling, and clear playbook organization. By leveraging Ansible's powerful automation capabilities, network administrators can manage large, complex networks more efficiently and effectively. Through the integration of monitoring tools, role-based configurations, and consistent configurations across devices, Ansible can ensure that networks remain reliable, secure, and scalable. With these strategies in place, Ansible provides a powerful framework for automating network management at scale, helping organizations maintain operational efficiency even as their networks continue to grow.

Leveraging Ansible Tower for Network Automation

As networks continue to grow in complexity, the need for automation in managing network devices and configurations becomes even more critical. Ansible, as an open-source automation platform, has been widely adopted for its simplicity, flexibility, and powerful features. However, when managing large-scale, enterprise-level networks, administrators require tools that offer enhanced capabilities such as centralized management, user access control, and visual reporting. Ansible Tower, the enterprise version of Ansible, addresses these needs by providing a more robust and user-friendly interface for managing automation workflows. By leveraging Ansible Tower for network automation, organizations can streamline their operations, improve efficiency, and ensure consistency across their network infrastructure.

Ansible Tower serves as a centralized hub for managing and orchestrating Ansible automation tasks. It builds on the core functionality of Ansible by offering a web-based interface, role-based access control, and integrated scheduling and reporting features. This makes it an ideal solution for large organizations and network teams that need to manage complex automation workflows across multiple teams, devices, and environments. With Ansible Tower, network administrators can manage playbooks, inventories, and job templates with ease, ensuring that their network automation processes are executed efficiently and securely.

One of the primary advantages of using Ansible Tower for network automation is its centralized management capabilities. In large networks with hundreds or even thousands of devices, managing Ansible playbooks and inventory files can become cumbersome and prone to errors. Ansible Tower allows administrators to store and organize playbooks, inventories, and variables in a centralized location, making it easier to manage and update automation tasks. Playbooks can be organized into templates, which can be reused and shared across different teams and projects. This centralized approach not only simplifies the management of automation workflows but also ensures that configurations are consistent and up to date across the entire network.

Ansible Tower also provides a more user-friendly interface for managing network automation tasks. While Ansible itself is powerful, its command-line interface can be difficult for some network administrators to navigate, especially those who may not be familiar with programming or scripting. Ansible Tower's web-based interface allows administrators to interact with their automation tasks through an intuitive graphical user interface (GUI). This makes it easier to create, modify, and run playbooks, as well as monitor the status of ongoing jobs. Additionally, the interface provides detailed logs and error messages, making it simpler to troubleshoot issues when they arise. This user-friendly design makes Ansible Tower an accessible solution for both experienced network engineers and those who are new to automation.

Role-based access control (RBAC) is another important feature of Ansible Tower that enhances security and operational efficiency in large network environments. In organizations with multiple teams and users, it is crucial to ensure that the right individuals have the appropriate level of access to sensitive network configurations and automation tasks. Ansible Tower allows administrators to define roles and assign permissions based on user responsibilities. This ensures that only authorized users can execute specific playbooks, access certain inventories, or modify configurations. By implementing RBAC, network administrators can enforce security policies, prevent unauthorized changes, and reduce the risk of human error. RBAC also helps in auditing and tracking changes, as it enables organizations to monitor who is making changes and when, providing a clear history of automation activities.

In addition to RBAC, Ansible Tower provides integrated scheduling capabilities, allowing network administrators to automate tasks on a defined schedule. For example, tasks such as network configuration backups, software updates, or security patches can be scheduled to run at regular intervals or during off-peak hours to minimize disruptions to network services. Scheduling these tasks through Ansible Tower ensures that critical maintenance activities are performed on time and consistently, without requiring manual intervention. This level of automation not only saves time but also helps maintain the health and security of the network by ensuring that essential tasks are not overlooked.

Another significant advantage of Ansible Tower for network automation is its ability to scale and integrate with other tools and systems. Large organizations often have complex network architectures with devices from various vendors, as well as third-party systems for monitoring, logging, and ticketing. Ansible Tower can integrate with these systems to create a seamless automation workflow. For example, Ansible Tower can be integrated with network monitoring tools to automatically respond to network events, such as device failures or performance degradation. When a problem is detected, Ansible Tower can automatically trigger an automation playbook to resolve the issue, such as rebooting a device or applying a configuration change. This integration allows for a more dynamic and responsive network automation environment, where actions are triggered based on real-time data and events.

Ansible Tower also supports the management of large-scale inventories, making it ideal for networks with numerous devices. In large networks, keeping track of devices, their roles, and configurations can be challenging. Ansible Tower simplifies this process by allowing administrators to define and manage inventories of devices and groups. Devices can be organized into logical groups based on factors such as location, device type, or role within the network. This grouping helps to streamline the management of devices, as playbooks can be targeted at specific groups rather than having to define devices individually. Furthermore, dynamic inventory support in Ansible Tower allows for automatic updates to inventories based on changes in the network, such as the addition of new devices or the removal of obsolete ones.

For network monitoring and reporting, Ansible Tower offers advanced capabilities that are essential for tracking the progress of automation tasks and ensuring that network configurations are applied correctly. The built-in reporting functionality provides detailed insights into the status of jobs, including success rates, failure reasons, and performance metrics. This helps network administrators quickly identify issues, assess the impact of automation tasks, and ensure that configurations are applied as expected. Reports can be generated for specific tasks or playbooks, and they can be used for auditing purposes to track changes over time. Ansible Tower also integrates with external reporting tools, enabling administrators to incorporate network automation data into broader reporting frameworks or dashboards.

One of the key features that sets Ansible Tower apart is its ability to handle complex workflows and dependencies. In large networks, automation tasks often need to be performed in a specific sequence, with certain tasks dependent on the successful completion of others. Ansible Tower allows administrators to define job workflows that can include multiple playbooks, conditional logic, and error handling. For example, if a configuration change requires a device reboot, Ansible Tower can be configured to automatically check the status of the device before proceeding with the next task. This level of orchestration ensures that automation tasks are executed in the correct order and that errors are handled appropriately.

The scalability of Ansible Tower is another factor that makes it an ideal solution for large networks. As organizations expand their networks, they need an automation platform that can handle increasing demands. Ansible Tower can scale horizontally by adding additional instances to support larger workloads and more devices. This ensures that network automation can keep up with the growing needs of the network, whether it is managing more devices, executing more complex tasks, or handling more frequent automation jobs.

Leveraging Ansible Tower for network automation provides organizations with a powerful tool for managing complex network infrastructures. Through centralized management, role-based access control, scheduling, and integration with other systems, Ansible Tower enhances the capabilities of Ansible and makes network automation more efficient, secure, and scalable. By providing a user-friendly interface, detailed reporting, and advanced workflow management, Ansible Tower simplifies the process of automating network operations, reducing manual intervention and minimizing errors. As networks continue to grow in size and complexity, Ansible Tower provides the necessary tools to manage them effectively, ensuring that network operations remain smooth, secure, and efficient.

Automating VPN Configuration with NETCONF

Virtual Private Networks (VPNs) have become a crucial part of modern network architectures, providing secure communication channels between remote devices and corporate networks. Whether used for site-to-site connectivity, remote user access, or cloud interconnection, VPNs play an essential role in maintaining data privacy and security. However, as network environments become increasingly complex and distributed, managing VPN configurations manually can become a cumbersome and error-prone process. NETCONF, a network management protocol, offers an automated solution to streamline VPN configuration tasks. By leveraging NETCONF for automating VPN setups, network engineers can significantly reduce human error, increase efficiency, and ensure consistency across devices.

NETCONF, or Network Configuration Protocol, is a protocol developed for automating network device configurations, and it allows administrators to manage network configurations programmatically. It operates by using Extensible Markup Language (XML) to request, retrieve, and configure device settings. NETCONF is widely used for managing devices that support YANG data models, which provide a structured approach to representing device configuration data. When it comes to VPN configuration, NETCONF simplifies the task by enabling the automation of processes like tunnel creation, encryption settings, and routing configuration. This is particularly valuable for large networks where VPNs are used across many devices and locations.

The traditional approach to VPN configuration often involves manual input of configuration commands on each device. This process can be time-consuming, especially when dealing with large numbers of devices or making updates across multiple sites. Furthermore, human errors in manual configuration can lead to misconfigurations, resulting in connectivity issues or security vulnerabilities. By using NETCONF, network engineers can automate these tasks, ensuring that VPN settings are consistently applied across the network. This not only saves time but also improves the reliability and security of the VPN configurations.

Automating VPN configuration with NETCONF begins with defining the desired VPN settings within a structured configuration file. The configuration includes parameters such as the VPN type (e.g., IPsec, SSL VPN), tunnel endpoints, encryption algorithms, and authentication methods. These parameters are then translated into YANG data models, which are used by NETCONF to communicate with network devices. Once the configuration is defined, NETCONF can push these settings to the target devices, ensuring that the VPN configuration is applied consistently across the network. This process eliminates the need for manual intervention and reduces the chances of human error.

In practice, NETCONF's automation capabilities extend to various aspects of VPN management. For example, administrators can automate the creation of IPsec tunnels between remote sites by defining the tunnel parameters in a playbook. This can include the IP addresses of the tunnel endpoints, the security protocols to be used (such as IKEv2 or IPSec), and the authentication credentials for the remote devices. Once the configuration is defined, NETCONF can automatically apply the settings to each device, establishing the VPN tunnel without the need for manual intervention. This automation can be extended to include other VPN-related tasks, such as configuring routing for the tunnel, adjusting access control lists (ACLs), and setting up Network Address Translation (NAT) for VPN traffic.

One of the key benefits of using NETCONF for automating VPN configuration is its ability to work with multiple vendors' devices in a standardized manner. In many networks, devices from different manufacturers are used, each with their own configuration syntax and methods for setting up VPNs. NETCONF, in combination with YANG data models, abstracts away these differences and provides a unified approach to managing VPN configurations. This means that a single NETCONF playbook can be used to configure VPNs across devices from multiple vendors, reducing the complexity of managing a multi-vendor network. Additionally, the use of YANG data models ensures that configurations are expressed in a standardized format, making it easier to maintain and troubleshoot VPN setups across the network.

NETCONF's ability to automate VPN configuration also enhances scalability. As networks grow and new remote sites or devices are added, VPN configuration can quickly become a logistical challenge. With NETCONF, adding new VPN connections becomes a matter of updating the configuration files and running the playbook to apply the changes. This makes it easier to scale the network and maintain VPN connections across a large number of devices. Furthermore, NETCONF can be used to automate the provisioning of new VPN connections for remote users, ensuring that they are set up quickly and consistently.

Another significant advantage of automating VPN configuration with NETCONF is the ability to perform configuration validation and verification. When configuring VPNs manually, there is always the risk of misconfiguring critical settings, such as encryption methods or tunnel endpoints, which can result in connectivity failures or security vulnerabilities. NETCONF allows administrators to validate the configuration before applying it, ensuring that all required parameters are correctly defined and that there are no conflicts between settings. Additionally, NETCONF can be used to periodically verify the configuration of VPNs, checking for compliance with security policies and identifying any deviations from the desired state. This helps ensure that VPNs remain secure and operational, even as the network evolves.

NETCONF also integrates well with other automation tools and monitoring systems, which enhances its value in large networks. For example, NETCONF can be used in conjunction with monitoring tools to automatically adjust VPN configurations based on network conditions. If a network performance issue is detected, such as high latency or packet loss, NETCONF can be used to modify the VPN configuration to adjust routing paths, encryption algorithms, or other parameters to improve performance. This level of integration allows for more dynamic and responsive network management, where VPN configurations are automatically adapted to changing network conditions. Furthermore, NETCONF's ability to integrate with centralized logging and alerting systems enables administrators to track changes to VPN configurations and receive alerts when issues arise.

The use of NETCONF for automating VPN configuration also contributes to improved security. VPNs are critical to protecting sensitive data and ensuring secure communication across the network. By automating VPN setup with NETCONF, administrators can ensure that the correct security settings, such as encryption methods and authentication protocols, are consistently applied across all devices. This reduces the risk of misconfigurations that could lead to vulnerabilities or breaches. Furthermore, because NETCONF is built on secure transport protocols like SSH, the automation process itself is secure, ensuring that configuration changes are transmitted and applied safely.

NETCONF's role in automating VPN configuration can also be extended to the management of VPN performance. As network traffic grows, administrators need to ensure that VPNs are performing optimally, with minimal latency and maximum throughput. NETCONF can be used to automate the collection of performance metrics related to VPN tunnels, such as bandwidth usage and tunnel uptime. This data can then be used to identify potential issues, optimize configurations, and ensure that the VPN infrastructure is meeting performance requirements. Automated monitoring and performance tuning are essential for maintaining the reliability and efficiency of VPNs, especially in large-scale environments.

By leveraging NETCONF for automating VPN configuration, organizations can significantly reduce the complexity of managing secure network connections. The ability to define, configure, and verify VPN settings programmatically not only saves time but also ensures that configurations are consistently applied across the network. NETCONF's integration with other network management tools and its ability to work across multiple vendor devices make it an ideal solution for large, heterogeneous networks. Whether for site-to-site VPNs, remote user access, or inter-cloud connectivity, automating VPN configuration with NETCONF provides organizations with a powerful tool for improving network security, scalability, and performance.

Managing Quality of Service (QoS) with Ansible

Quality of Service (QoS) is a crucial aspect of network management, ensuring that different types of traffic receive appropriate levels of service based on their priority. In environments where multiple applications and services share the same network resources, managing QoS effectively is essential for optimizing network performance and maintaining service quality. QoS allows network administrators to prioritize critical applications, allocate bandwidth efficiently, and reduce latency or packet loss, especially for real-time services such as VoIP, video conferencing, and online gaming. However, implementing and maintaining QoS policies across a large and dynamic network can be complex and time-consuming. This is where automation tools like Ansible come into play. By leveraging Ansible to manage QoS configurations, network administrators can simplify the process, reduce human error, and ensure consistency across their network infrastructure.

Ansible is an open-source automation tool designed to automate IT tasks such as configuration management, application deployment, and network provisioning. It uses simple, human-readable YAML files called playbooks to define tasks that can be executed on network devices and servers. One of Ansible's strengths is its ability to work with a variety of network devices, from routers and switches to firewalls and load balancers, using specialized modules. These modules can interact with network devices via protocols like SSH or NETCONF, enabling the automation of complex configuration tasks such as managing QoS policies.

Managing QoS with Ansible begins with understanding the QoS requirements of the network. Different applications and services have varying needs in terms of bandwidth, latency, jitter, and packet loss. For example, real-time voice and video traffic require low latency and high priority, while file transfers and email services can tolerate higher latency and lower priority. Ansible allows network administrators to automate the creation and enforcement of QoS policies based on these requirements, ensuring that each application or service receives the appropriate level of service.

Ansible provides several network modules that can be used to manage QoS on devices like Cisco routers, Juniper switches, and other network equipment. The modules, such as ios_qos_policy for Cisco devices, allow administrators to define traffic classes, apply traffic shaping, configure policing and scheduling policies, and set up congestion management. These modules are designed to work with the native QoS mechanisms supported by the devices, enabling administrators to automate the application of QoS policies across the network with minimal manual intervention. For example, with Ansible, administrators can configure DiffServ (Differentiated Services) or IP Precedence markings, define class maps, and associate them with traffic policies such as bandwidth allocation or drop thresholds.

One of the key benefits of using Ansible for QoS management is its ability to enforce consistency across the network. In a large network with numerous routers and switches, manually applying QoS settings can be error-prone, especially when configurations must be replicated across multiple devices. With Ansible, network engineers can define QoS policies as part of a playbook, which can then be applied to multiple devices simultaneously. This approach ensures that QoS configurations are applied consistently across the network, reducing the risk of configuration discrepancies and ensuring that the network performs optimally for all users and applications.

Another advantage of using Ansible for managing QoS is its ability to simplify the modification and updates of QoS policies. In dynamic network environments, network conditions and requirements change frequently. For instance, an organization may need to adjust its QoS policies to accommodate new applications or prioritize different types of traffic. Traditionally, making changes to QoS settings across a large network would involve manually editing configurations on each device, which is time-consuming and prone to errors. With Ansible, administrators can modify the playbooks to reflect the new QoS requirements, and the updated configuration can be applied across the entire network in a single execution. This not only saves time but also ensures that changes are applied uniformly, reducing the risk of inconsistency.

Ansible's ability to work with various devices and vendors is another significant advantage when managing QoS. Networks often consist of devices from multiple manufacturers, each with its own configuration syntax and QoS implementation. Ansible's modular architecture allows administrators to define a single, standardized set of QoS policies that can be applied to different types of devices, whether they are Cisco, Juniper, or Arista. For example, administrators can write a playbook that applies the same traffic shaping policy across devices from different vendors, ensuring that the network operates seamlessly regardless of the hardware in use. This is especially important in large, multi-vendor networks, where consistency across diverse devices is essential for maintaining service quality.

Beyond defining and applying QoS policies, Ansible can also be used to monitor and verify the performance of QoS configurations. In a network, it is essential to ensure that the applied QoS settings are functioning as intended. Ansible allows administrators to automate the process of collecting data on traffic flows, bandwidth utilization, and congestion levels across the network. This data can then be used to verify whether the QoS policies are being enforced correctly. For instance, Ansible can query network devices for interface statistics, such as the number of packets dropped or the amount of bandwidth used by high-priority traffic. If any issues are detected, administrators can modify the playbooks and apply the updated configuration to resolve the problem.

Ansible also supports the automation of QoS monitoring and reporting, allowing network administrators to track the effectiveness of their QoS policies over time. With automated reporting, administrators can receive regular updates on the performance of the network, including how well traffic is being prioritized and whether any bottlenecks or congestion issues are emerging. This information is critical for maintaining a high level of service quality and ensuring that QoS settings are adjusted as needed to meet evolving network demands.

In addition to performance monitoring, Ansible's integration with other IT management tools makes it easier to incorporate QoS configuration into broader network management strategies. For example, Ansible can be integrated with network monitoring and alerting systems to automatically trigger QoS policy adjustments based on real-time network conditions. If a monitoring system detects that a particular application is experiencing network congestion, Ansible can automatically adjust the QoS settings to prioritize that traffic. This level of automation helps create a dynamic network that can adapt to changing conditions, improving overall performance and reliability.

Managing QoS with Ansible also brings scalability to network management. As networks expand, it becomes increasingly difficult to manage QoS policies manually, especially when dealing with large numbers of devices. Ansible's ability to automate QoS configurations across multiple devices simplifies the management of large networks. Whether an organization is adding new devices, expanding its network, or deploying new applications, Ansible allows administrators to quickly implement consistent QoS settings across the entire network. This scalability ensures that QoS management remains efficient and effective, even as the network grows.

Using Ansible to manage QoS not only enhances the network's performance but also improves the overall network security and reliability. By automating the application of QoS policies, organizations can ensure that critical traffic is prioritized, reducing the likelihood of performance degradation or service disruptions. Moreover, automation reduces the risk of human error, ensuring that QoS settings are consistently applied according to best practices. With Ansible, network administrators can more effectively manage the complexities of QoS, ensuring that applications and services perform optimally and that the network remains reliable and secure.

In summary, Ansible provides a powerful and efficient solution for managing Quality of Service in modern networks. Through automation, administrators can define, apply, and monitor QoS policies consistently across a wide variety of devices and vendors. By simplifying QoS management, Ansible helps organizations maintain high network performance, prioritize critical applications, and ensure the reliability of their network infrastructure.

Using Ansible for Network Device Health Checks

Maintaining the health and performance of network devices is an ongoing challenge for network administrators, particularly in large and dynamic environments where hundreds or even thousands of devices are in operation. Whether it's a router, switch, firewall, or other network infrastructure device, ensuring that each piece of equipment is functioning optimally is essential for maintaining a stable and secure network. Traditional methods of performing health checks, which often involve manual inspection or sporadic device monitoring, can be time-consuming, error-prone, and ineffective at scale. This is where Ansible, an open-source automation tool, can play a pivotal role. By leveraging Ansible for network device health checks, network administrators can automate the process of monitoring device performance, identifying issues, and ensuring the overall health of the network infrastructure in a more efficient and consistent manner.

Ansible is widely used for network automation, primarily for its ability to execute playbooks across a diverse set of devices and environments. Using Ansible for network device health checks allows administrators to automate tasks such as retrieving device status, checking resource utilization, and verifying configurations without manual intervention. By automating these health checks, organizations can ensure that potential issues are identified early, often before they escalate into significant problems, thus improving network reliability and minimizing downtime.

The first step in using Ansible for network device health checks is to define the specific health parameters that need to be monitored. These can include a wide range of metrics, such as CPU and memory utilization, interface status, temperature readings, fan speeds, and even error rates on network interfaces. The beauty of Ansible lies in its flexibility, as administrators can define custom health check parameters based on the specific needs of their network devices. For example, for routers and switches, one might want to monitor the number of dropped packets, interface up/down status, and CPU load, while for firewalls, one might monitor firewall rule health or throughput statistics. Ansible allows administrators to tailor these checks to meet the unique needs of their network infrastructure.

Once the relevant health parameters are identified, Ansible can be used to automate the collection of this information from network devices. Ansible offers a variety of modules designed to work with different networking platforms, including Cisco, Juniper, and Arista devices. These modules can be used to execute commands on network devices and gather real-time data related to device health. For example, the ios_facts module for Cisco devices can collect operational data such as device uptime, interface status, and memory usage, while the junos_facts module for Juniper devices can retrieve similar information. The collected data can then be used for further analysis and decision-making.

Ansible playbooks are at the heart of automating network device health checks. A typical playbook to check the health of network devices would contain tasks that retrieve data from multiple devices in parallel, ensuring that the health of each device is assessed quickly and efficiently. These tasks might include retrieving interface statistics, checking for errors or packet drops, verifying CPU and memory usage, and gathering information about the device's overall status. Once the data is collected, it can be parsed and processed within the playbook to identify any potential issues. For example, the playbook can be configured to generate alerts when CPU usage exceeds a certain threshold or when an interface is down for an extended period of time. This approach reduces the need for manual health checks and allows network administrators to monitor large numbers of devices simultaneously.

One of the key benefits of using Ansible for network device health checks is its ability to perform these checks regularly and at scale. In large networks, manually checking the health of each device on a frequent basis can be impractical. With Ansible, administrators can schedule playbooks to run at regular intervals, ensuring that device health is continuously monitored. For example, a playbook can be scheduled to run daily or weekly to check the health of all devices in the network. This proactive approach to monitoring means that potential issues are identified early and addressed before they affect network performance. It also reduces the burden on network administrators, freeing up time to focus on more critical tasks.

Another significant advantage of using Ansible for device health checks is the ability to integrate these checks with other monitoring and alerting systems. Ansible can be integrated with tools such as Nagios, Zabbix, or custom-built monitoring systems to trigger alerts based on the results of health checks. If a device is found to be experiencing issues, such as high CPU usage or an interface going down, Ansible can automatically notify administrators via email, SMS, or other communication channels. This real-time alerting mechanism allows for quicker response times and ensures that network issues are addressed promptly. Furthermore, Ansible can be configured to take corrective actions automatically if a health check fails. For instance, if an interface is found to be down, Ansible could be used to automatically reboot the device or reset the interface, minimizing the time the network is affected by the failure.

In addition to identifying and alerting on issues, Ansible can be used to automate the remediation of certain health problems. For example, if a network device's CPU usage exceeds a threshold for a certain period, Ansible can be programmed to automatically perform specific actions to alleviate the issue. These actions might include restarting certain services, reloading configurations, or adjusting device settings to reduce resource consumption. This automated remediation process not only reduces the need for manual intervention but also ensures that the network remains operational with minimal downtime.

Ansible also makes it easy to scale health checks across large networks. With hundreds or thousands of devices in a network, manually checking each device's health is not feasible. Ansible's ability to execute tasks in parallel allows administrators to monitor multiple devices at once, significantly reducing the time and effort required to perform health checks. This parallelism ensures that large networks can be monitored efficiently without compromising performance or accuracy. Ansible's inventory system further simplifies scaling by allowing administrators to define device groups, making it easier to apply health checks to different sets of devices, whether they are grouped by location, device type, or function within the network.

Moreover, Ansible's integration with version control systems like Git allows administrators to track changes to their health check configurations and ensure that any modifications to health check tasks are properly versioned and audited. This makes it easier to maintain consistency across a network, particularly when updates to health check tasks are required. With Ansible, administrators can quickly deploy updated configurations across multiple devices, ensuring that all devices are monitored according to the latest policies and standards.

One of the major strengths of using Ansible for network device health checks is its ability to provide a comprehensive overview of network performance. Rather than relying on disparate monitoring tools and manual processes, Ansible consolidates health check tasks into a single platform, making it easier for administrators to gather, analyze, and respond to network performance data. The results of these health checks can be logged, stored, and even visualized through dashboards, providing a holistic view of network health over time. This data-driven approach helps administrators spot trends, anticipate potential issues, and make informed decisions about network maintenance and upgrades.

In summary, using Ansible for network device health checks offers a streamlined and automated approach to monitoring the performance and status of network devices. By automating the process of collecting, analyzing, and responding to device health data, Ansible helps network administrators ensure that their infrastructure remains reliable and efficient. From scheduling regular checks and generating real-time alerts to performing automated remediation, Ansible empowers administrators to proactively manage network health at scale, reducing downtime and improving the overall performance of the network.

NETCONF Filters and XPath for Fine-Grained Control

Network management protocols have become increasingly vital in large and complex network environments, and NETCONF (Network Configuration Protocol) is one of the most widely used tools for automating and managing network device configurations. NETCONF allows administrators to manage network devices in a standardized manner, enabling configuration, monitoring, and retrieval of device data. While NETCONF provides powerful functionality for interacting with network devices, its true potential is realized when coupled with filters and XPath expressions. These tools provide network administrators with fine-grained control over the data they retrieve and modify, offering flexibility and efficiency in managing large-scale networks. Filters and XPath are key features of NETCONF, helping to define and refine the information that is communicated between network management systems and network devices.

At its core, NETCONF uses XML as the primary data format for configuration and operational data exchange. This XML structure can be extremely large and detailed, as network devices often contain a wealth of configuration settings and performance metrics. When querying a network device using NETCONF, an administrator may not need to retrieve the entire dataset but rather just a specific part of it. This is where filters and XPath come into play. Filters allow administrators to specify which parts of the data they are interested in, reducing the amount of information exchanged and making the process more efficient. XPath, a powerful query language designed to navigate through XML documents, provides a flexible and precise way to extract exactly the data required.

Using filters in NETCONF allows administrators to narrow down their requests to only the data they need. Filters can be defined in the NETCONF request to limit the scope of the query, ensuring that only relevant information is retrieved. This is especially useful when working with devices that have large configuration files or when only specific attributes are of interest. For example, an administrator may want to retrieve only the interface statistics or only the configuration of certain routing protocols, rather than pulling the entire device configuration. By applying a filter, the query can focus on these specific elements, saving time and processing resources.

Filters in NETCONF are defined using a simple XML-based format. When performing a <get> operation to retrieve data, an administrator can include a <filter> element in the request to specify which parts of the configuration should be returned. The filter element can contain specific XPath expressions or references to data models that define the structure of the information. These filters allow for precise control over the data that is returned from the device, making it possible to query specific configuration parameters or operational statistics without the need to retrieve extraneous information.

XPath enhances this filtering capability by allowing administrators to define sophisticated queries to extract specific data from XML documents. XPath is a language that provides a way to navigate and query XML documents, making it an ideal tool for interacting with NETCONF's XML-based data structure. With XPath, administrators can specify complex criteria for retrieving information, such as selecting data based on specific attributes or values. This gives administrators a level of control that is not possible with basic filters alone. For instance, XPath can be used to select all interfaces with a specific status, such as "up" or "down," or to retrieve data from a particular VLAN or subnet.

The power of XPath lies in its ability to traverse XML documents in a flexible and dynamic manner. XPath supports a range of functions that allow administrators to refine their queries, such as selecting nodes based on conditions, filtering data by values, and extracting data based on relationships between elements in the document. For example, an administrator could use XPath to select only those interface statistics where the number of errors exceeds a certain threshold, providing a focused view of the network's health. This level of granularity is especially valuable when dealing with large-scale networks, where the volume of data is substantial, and administrators need a way to zoom in on the most critical or relevant information.

One of the most powerful features of combining NETCONF filters with XPath is the ability to perform hierarchical queries. Network device configurations are often structured in a hierarchical manner, with different levels of configuration nested under broader categories. For example, a network device might have a top-level configuration for interfaces, under which there are specific settings for each interface. With XPath, administrators can traverse this hierarchy and select specific configurations or operational data from within these nested structures. This capability allows for more targeted queries and more efficient data retrieval, as administrators can focus on a particular device feature or component rather than retrieving all the data in a given category.

Another significant benefit of using filters and XPath with NETCONF is the ability to streamline data retrieval when working with large networks or multiple devices. In a large network, retrieving complete configuration data from every device can be time-consuming and resource-intensive. By using filters to limit the scope of the data and XPath to define specific data points, administrators can significantly reduce the amount of information transferred across the network. This not only improves efficiency but also helps to reduce network congestion and ensure that the management system operates smoothly even with large amounts of data.

Filters and XPath are not limited to read-only operations but can also be used to modify device configurations. In NETCONF, administrators can send configuration changes to a device using the <edit-config> operation. When making these changes, filters and XPath can be used to identify which parts of the configuration need to be updated. For example, if an administrator wants to modify the settings of a specific interface, they can use an XPath expression to target the interface's configuration and update the necessary parameters without affecting other parts of the device's configuration. This precision reduces the risk of accidental misconfigurations and ensures that only the desired changes are made.

In addition to their use in configuration management, filters and XPath can also be employed in the monitoring and troubleshooting of network devices. When troubleshooting issues, administrators may need to retrieve specific performance data, such as interface error counts, routing table entries, or CPU utilization. By using filters and XPath, administrators can quickly and efficiently retrieve only the relevant data, enabling faster identification of the problem. This targeted approach improves the overall speed and effectiveness of network troubleshooting, reducing downtime and improving network reliability.

Integrating filters and XPath into NETCONF requests also enhances automation workflows. In large-scale networks, automation is key to maintaining consistency and reducing the workload of network administrators. By incorporating filters and XPath into automation playbooks, administrators can create more efficient and intelligent automation workflows that dynamically query and modify device configurations based on specific criteria. For example, an automated script could be created to check the status of network interfaces across multiple devices and automatically adjust QoS settings or routing protocols based on the retrieved data. This automation not only saves time but also ensures that network changes are applied consistently and in real-time.

The flexibility provided by filters and XPath within the NETCONF framework makes it a powerful tool for managing network configurations and monitoring device health. By allowing administrators to define exactly which data to retrieve and modify, these tools enhance the efficiency, accuracy, and scalability of network management. Whether managing large networks, troubleshooting issues, or automating configuration changes, filters and XPath provide the fine-grained control that is essential for maintaining optimal network performance. As network environments continue to grow in size and complexity, the need for precise, efficient management tools like NETCONF will only become more critical. Filters and XPath are integral to this process, enabling network administrators to handle vast amounts of data with ease and ensuring that network configurations are consistently optimized.

Troubleshooting NETCONF and Ansible Integration

The integration of NETCONF with Ansible has become an essential solution for network automation, enabling administrators to manage network devices more efficiently and effectively. NETCONF, a network management protocol, allows administrators to configure and monitor network devices in a standardized way, while Ansible, an automation tool, provides a simple and powerful platform for automating IT tasks. Together, these tools offer the ability to automate network configuration, monitoring, and maintenance across large-scale environments. However, like any complex system, troubleshooting NETCONF and Ansible integration can pose challenges. Whether it's a connectivity issue, a misconfiguration, or an unexpected behavior in the automated workflows, understanding how to identify and resolve issues is key to maintaining a reliable and efficient automation environment.

One of the first common issues that administrators face when troubleshooting NETCONF and Ansible integration is connectivity problems between Ansible and the network devices. NETCONF typically communicates with devices over SSH, which means that any connectivity issues between the Ansible control machine and the network devices will prevent successful interaction. Connectivity problems may arise due to incorrect IP addresses, network misconfigurations, or firewall settings blocking the necessary ports. In many cases, the issue can be traced back to simple network problems, such as an unreachable device or incorrect routing. To address this, administrators should first verify the network connectivity to the devices using basic network troubleshooting tools, such as ping and traceroute, before diving deeper into the configuration of NETCONF or Ansible.

Another key area of troubleshooting involves verifying the correct configuration of the NETCONF protocol on the network devices themselves. NETCONF is supported by many modern network devices, but it requires the protocol to be explicitly enabled. If NETCONF is not enabled on the device, or if the necessary ports are not open, NETCONF requests from Ansible will fail. It is important to ensure that the device is correctly configured to support NETCONF, which typically involves enabling the protocol in the device's configuration and ensuring that the appropriate authentication methods (such as SSH keys or usernames and passwords) are configured correctly. If the device is properly configured but issues persist, it may be necessary to check device logs for any error messages related to NETCONF and investigate whether there are any specific limitations or incompatibilities with the version of NETCONF supported by the device.

Ansible playbooks, which define the automation tasks, can also be a source of problems when integrating with NETCONF. Ansible uses specific modules for interacting with network devices, such as ios_config for Cisco devices or junos_config for Juniper devices. These modules rely on the correct configuration of both the playbooks and the device to execute commands successfully. A common issue arises when the playbook is incorrectly written or contains syntax errors, leading to failures during execution. Ansible provides detailed error messages, but interpreting these messages requires a solid understanding of both the underlying NETCONF protocol and the specifics of the device configuration. Administrators should carefully review the playbook for syntax errors, missing parameters, or incorrect task definitions. In some cases, the error may be related to a mismatch in the expected configuration between the playbook and the actual device configuration, which can be resolved by updating the playbook to reflect the current device state.

Another issue that can arise during the integration of NETCONF and Ansible is incorrect handling of authentication and authorization. NETCONF relies on secure communication channels, typically SSH, and requires proper authentication to ensure secure access to the network devices. When troubleshooting, it is important to ensure that Ansible is using the correct credentials for accessing the devices. This includes verifying that the correct SSH keys are provided, ensuring that the Ansible control machine has access to these keys, and checking that the user account has the appropriate permissions on the network device. Misconfigured authentication settings can lead to errors that prevent Ansible from interacting with devices through NETCONF. Administrators should also verify that the devices are configured to accept the correct form of authentication, such as public key or password-based authentication, and ensure that the credentials provided in the Ansible inventory file or playbook match what is configured on the device.

Issues with the execution environment can also hinder the integration of NETCONF and Ansible. The Ansible control machine needs to have the appropriate dependencies installed to work with NETCONF. This includes ensuring that the required Python libraries and NETCONF-related modules are present. If the environment is missing any of these components, Ansible may fail to execute the required tasks. For instance, the ncclient library, which is commonly used for NETCONF communication in Python, must be installed and correctly configured. If the required libraries are missing or not properly installed, administrators will encounter errors when attempting to run playbooks that interact with NETCONF-enabled devices. Checking the Ansible control machine's environment and installing or updating the necessary dependencies is a critical troubleshooting step to ensure that the integration between Ansible and NETCONF works smoothly.

Timeouts are another common issue that can occur when integrating NETCONF with Ansible. Timeout errors often happen when the network device takes too long to respond to a request, such as a configuration change or a data retrieval command. This could be due to network congestion, device performance issues, or excessive load on the network device. In these cases, Ansible may report a timeout error, which can be frustrating for administrators. Adjusting the timeout settings in the playbook or Ansible configuration can help mitigate these issues. Additionally, reviewing the network device's performance and logs can provide insights into whether the device is under heavy load or experiencing other issues that may be causing delays in processing the NETCONF requests.

Another aspect of troubleshooting NETCONF and Ansible integration is ensuring that the correct data models are used for configuration and monitoring. NETCONF relies on YANG models to define the structure of the configuration data, and Ansible modules typically use these models to interact with the devices. If the YANG models are not correctly configured or if there is a version mismatch between the device's model and the version of Ansible being used, issues can arise. It is important to ensure that both the device and Ansible playbooks are using compatible YANG models. This may involve reviewing the device's YANG model version and ensuring that the correct version is referenced in the Ansible playbook or the associated modules.

When troubleshooting NETCONF and Ansible integration, it is also important to ensure that the devices being managed are running compatible versions of the NETCONF protocol. While NETCONF is widely supported across modern devices, different vendors may implement different versions of the protocol, and there can sometimes be differences in the supported features. In these cases, it may be necessary to update the device's software or firmware to ensure compatibility with the version of NETCONF that Ansible is using.

Ultimately, troubleshooting NETCONF and Ansible integration requires a systematic approach to identifying and resolving issues at various levels of the network management stack. From connectivity and authentication issues to misconfigured playbooks and network device settings, there are many potential causes of problems in this integration. By carefully reviewing the device configurations, Ansible playbooks, and execution environment, network administrators can identify the root cause of the issue and implement the necessary fixes. The flexibility and power of NETCONF and Ansible make them invaluable tools for network automation, and addressing integration challenges ensures that these tools can be used effectively to automate and manage large-scale network environments.

Leveraging Templates for Config Management in Ansible

In modern network automation, configuration management is crucial for ensuring consistency, efficiency, and scalability in network device setups. One of the most powerful features of Ansible for configuration management is the ability to leverage templates. Ansible uses Jinja2 templates, which allow for the dynamic generation of configuration files based on variables, conditions, and loops. This feature enables network administrators to automate the creation and management of complex network device configurations, ensuring that configurations are not only consistent but also easily adaptable to different environments or requirements. By using templates, administrators can reduce manual intervention, decrease the chance of errors, and improve the speed at which network configurations are deployed across large-scale environments.

Templates in Ansible are files that define configuration settings for network devices, where variables can be substituted dynamically during the execution of playbooks. These templates are written in Jinja2, a powerful templating engine used by Ansible to allow for dynamic content generation. Jinja2 supports a wide range of features, including variables, filters, loops, and conditional logic. This flexibility is what makes Ansible's templating system so powerful and useful in network configuration management. By defining templates, administrators can generate network device configurations that can easily be adapted to different devices, locations, or network roles without requiring manual intervention.

One of the primary benefits of using templates in Ansible for configuration management is the ability to centralize the configuration logic. Traditionally, network configurations are managed on a per-device basis, where each device's settings are manually written and updated. As the network grows, maintaining these configurations becomes more challenging, and the likelihood of errors increases. With Ansible templates, the configuration for multiple devices can be defined in a single template file, and variables can be substituted dynamically to generate device-specific configurations. This centralization ensures that configuration changes are made consistently across all devices, reducing the risk of errors and configuration drift.

Templates are particularly valuable when dealing with networks that span multiple locations or contain devices from different manufacturers. In such environments, configurations may need to vary slightly depending on the device type, role, or location. For instance, a router in one location might have a different IP addressing scheme than a router in another location, even though the core configuration (such as routing protocols or security settings) remains the same. By using templates, administrators can define the common configuration elements in one place and then customize them based on the device's specific requirements. The ability to inject variables into templates allows for the seamless creation of configuration files that are tailored to each device, minimizing manual work and reducing the chance of human error.

Ansible's templating system allows for the dynamic generation of configuration files, which is essential for managing complex network setups. For example, in a large network with hundreds of devices, each device might have its own set of interface configurations, IP addresses, or security policies. Writing these configurations manually for each device would be a tedious and error-prone process. Instead, administrators can define a template for the configuration file that includes placeholders for variables such as the device's hostname, IP address range, or interface settings. These variables can then be populated from Ansible's inventory or from other sources, ensuring that each device receives its specific configuration while maintaining consistency across the entire network.

Ansible's use of templates is particularly beneficial when dealing with dynamic environments. Networks are constantly changing, with devices being added, removed, or reconfigured on a regular basis. Manually updating configurations to reflect these changes can be time-consuming and error-prone. With templates, administrators can create flexible, reusable configuration files that automatically adjust to network changes. For example, if a new device is added to the network, the template can automatically include the necessary configuration for the new device, such as IP addresses, VLANs, and routing protocols, without requiring the administrator to manually write or update the configuration. This dynamic approach to configuration management allows networks to scale quickly and efficiently while maintaining consistency and accuracy.

Templates also make it easier to enforce network policies and standards. By using a single template to define network configurations, administrators can ensure that all devices adhere to the same policies, such as security settings, routing protocols, or interface configurations. If a policy change is required, such as updating a security protocol or changing the network addressing scheme, administrators can modify the template, and the changes will automatically be reflected across all devices that use the template. This ensures that network configurations remain standardized, which is crucial for maintaining security, performance, and reliability in large networks.

One of the challenges in large networks is the complexity of managing configurations for devices from different vendors. Network devices from different manufacturers may have different syntax or configuration conventions, making it difficult to apply a consistent configuration across the entire network. Ansible's templating system, combined with its extensive library of modules for different network vendors, simplifies this process by allowing administrators to define a common configuration template that can be adapted to different devices. For example, a template might include common elements like routing protocols or interface settings, with device-specific variables or syntax differences handled through conditional logic or vendor-specific modules. This flexibility makes it easier to manage multi-vendor environments and ensures that all devices are configured consistently, regardless of their manufacturer.

In addition to simplifying the creation and management of device configurations, Ansible templates also improve the troubleshooting process. When network issues arise, administrators can use the template-driven approach to quickly identify configuration discrepancies or errors. Since the configuration for each device is generated from a common template, any deviations from the expected configuration can be easily spotted and corrected. This consistency also makes it easier to audit configurations and track changes, as administrators can quickly compare the generated configuration files to the template to ensure that they match the desired state. By streamlining the troubleshooting and auditing processes, Ansible templates help to maintain network stability and reduce downtime.

Ansible templates are also valuable when it comes to configuration versioning and rollback. With network configurations defined in templates, administrators can track changes to the configuration over time and roll back to previous versions if necessary. This version control ensures that administrators have a clear history of configuration changes, which can be crucial for auditing purposes or troubleshooting issues caused by recent changes. If a new configuration causes problems, administrators can easily revert to an earlier version of the template and apply the previous configuration to restore network stability.

Using templates for configuration management in Ansible helps network administrators maintain efficient, consistent, and scalable management of network devices. Whether managing a small network or a large, multi-location environment, Ansible templates enable administrators to automate the creation and deployment of device configurations, reducing the risk of errors and improving the speed of deployment. The ability to centralize configuration logic, enforce network policies, and dynamically generate configurations based on device-specific variables offers flexibility and precision that is essential in today's fast-paced network environments. As networks continue to grow in complexity, the ability to leverage templates for configuration management will become even more crucial for ensuring that devices are configured correctly and that network performance is optimized.

Version Control for Network Automation Scripts

In the field of network automation, scripts are central to configuring, managing, and monitoring network devices. These scripts are often the backbone of automated network operations, helping to streamline tasks and reduce the complexity of large-scale environments. As networks become more sophisticated and the need for automation grows, maintaining and evolving these scripts becomes increasingly important. One of the key practices in ensuring the smooth development and deployment of network automation scripts is version control. Version control is a system that tracks changes to files, allowing network engineers to manage and track the evolution of their automation scripts over time. By integrating version control into network automation workflows, administrators can improve collaboration, enhance accountability, and ensure that automation scripts are maintained with a high level of accuracy and consistency.

Version control systems, such as Git, have become industry standards for managing software development projects, and they are equally beneficial when applied to network automation. These systems allow network engineers to track every modification made to a script, whether it is a small change to a configuration or a major update to an automation workflow. By using version control, teams can ensure that every change is logged, making it easier to identify when and why changes were made, who made them, and what the impact was. This historical record of changes is invaluable for troubleshooting issues, auditing configurations, and understanding the context behind network automation decisions.

One of the most significant benefits of using version control in network automation is the ability to collaborate effectively across teams. In large organizations, network automation scripts are often developed by multiple engineers working on different aspects of the network. Without a version control system, coordinating changes and ensuring that everyone is working with the latest version of the script can be cumbersome. Version control systems, like Git, enable multiple engineers to work on the same set of scripts simultaneously. Engineers can create branches to work on new features or fixes without interfering with each other's work. Once their changes are complete, they can merge their work into the main codebase, ensuring that all updates are incorporated and properly tested before deployment. This level of collaboration is essential for maintaining large automation projects and ensuring that scripts are developed and deployed efficiently.

In addition to improving collaboration, version control also enhances accountability within network automation teams. By tracking every change made to a script, version control systems provide a clear audit trail. This audit trail is crucial for understanding the evolution of network automation scripts, especially when issues arise. If a problem occurs in the network after a change to an automation script, administrators can easily review the version history to identify when the change was made, what was modified, and by whom. This level of transparency helps teams to quickly pinpoint the root cause of issues and take corrective actions. Furthermore, version control systems allow engineers to roll back changes to a previous state if necessary. If a new change causes a disruption or issue, the script can be reverted to a stable version, minimizing the downtime and potential impact on network operations.

Another important advantage of version control in network automation is the ability to manage and maintain a consistent configuration across a large network. In large environments with many devices and automation scripts, maintaining consistency can be a challenge. Version control ensures that the most up-to-date scripts are applied to all devices, preventing inconsistencies that could arise from manual configuration. By storing automation scripts in a version control repository, administrators can ensure that every device is using the correct version of the script, reducing the risk of misconfigurations or version mismatches. Additionally, version control makes it easier to manage different configurations for different environments. For example, an organization may have separate scripts for testing, staging, and production environments. With version control, administrators can easily switch between these configurations and ensure that the correct scripts are applied to the appropriate environments.

Version control also facilitates testing and validation of network automation scripts. In complex network environments, testing automation scripts before deployment is essential to ensure they work as expected and do not introduce any issues. With version control, administrators can use branches to create separate testing environments where new scripts can be developed, tested, and validated without affecting the production network. Once the testing is complete and the script is validated, it can be merged into the main branch and deployed across the network. This process helps to minimize the risk of errors and ensures that scripts are thoroughly tested before they are used in a live environment.

For organizations that employ continuous integration and continuous delivery (CI/CD) practices, version control is an integral part of automating the deployment of network automation scripts. CI/CD pipelines allow for the automatic testing, validation, and deployment of scripts as they are developed. Version control systems are the backbone of these pipelines, providing the foundation for automated processes to ensure that only tested and approved scripts are deployed to network devices. By integrating version control into the CI/CD pipeline, organizations can automate the entire process of network configuration management, from development to deployment, ensuring that scripts are always up-to-date and consistently applied across the network.

Security is another critical consideration in network automation, and version control plays a role in enhancing the security of automation scripts. When sensitive information, such as passwords or API keys, is included in automation scripts, it is important to manage these scripts securely to prevent unauthorized access. Version control systems can help mitigate the risk of security breaches by allowing administrators to track access to the repository and ensuring that only authorized users are able to make changes to the scripts. Additionally, version control systems allow engineers to review changes before they are merged into the main branch, ensuring that sensitive information is not inadvertently exposed. By securely managing automation scripts in a version control system, organizations can reduce the risk of security vulnerabilities and ensure that automation practices adhere to best practices for data protection.

Managing network automation scripts with version control also contributes to network configuration management best practices.

When scripts are stored and tracked in a version control system, it becomes easier to manage configuration drift, which occurs when network configurations deviate from the intended state over time. With version control, administrators can quickly compare the current state of the automation scripts with previous versions, identifying any discrepancies and addressing them before they cause issues. This capability is crucial for maintaining network stability and ensuring that all devices are configured according to the most current standards and policies.

Finally, version control for network automation scripts allows for greater flexibility and scalability in network management. As networks continue to evolve and expand, the automation scripts must also evolve to meet new requirements. By using version control, administrators can easily manage the growth and evolution of these scripts, ensuring that the network remains agile and adaptable to changing needs. Whether adding new devices, modifying configurations, or updating automation workflows, version control provides a robust framework for managing the complexity of modern network environments.

In the realm of network automation, version control is not just a best practice, but a necessity for ensuring that automation scripts are developed, maintained, and deployed effectively. By providing a centralized, transparent, and organized system for managing scripts, version control improves collaboration, accountability, consistency, and security. It allows network administrators to keep automation workflows running smoothly, minimize downtime, and ensure that network configurations are always accurate and up to date. As network environments grow more complex and automation becomes increasingly important, the role of version control in network automation will only continue to grow.

Automating BGP Configuration with Ansible

Border Gateway Protocol (BGP) is one of the most widely used routing protocols in large-scale networks, particularly for inter-domain routing. BGP plays a crucial role in the exchange of routing information between different networks or autonomous systems (ASes), and it is integral to the operation of the global internet. As networks become more complex and interconnected, managing BGP configurations manually can be error-prone and inefficient. This is where automation tools like Ansible can significantly improve the process. Ansible, an open-source automation platform, can be used to automate the configuration, management, and monitoring of BGP settings across multiple devices, simplifying the process and reducing the risk of configuration errors. By leveraging Ansible for BGP configuration, network administrators can ensure consistency, scalability, and efficiency in their network operations.

Ansible is a powerful automation tool that uses playbooks written in YAML (Yet Another Markup Language) to define a series of tasks that can be executed on remote devices. These tasks can automate a wide range of network configuration tasks, from setting up interfaces to configuring routing protocols like BGP. Ansible supports many network vendors, including Cisco, Juniper, and Arista, which makes it an ideal tool for automating BGP configurations in multi-vendor environments. By using Ansible to automate the process of configuring BGP, network engineers can reduce the manual effort required to set up and maintain BGP across multiple routers or switches, ensuring that network changes are applied consistently and reliably.

To begin automating BGP configuration with Ansible, administrators first need to define the BGP settings that need to be configured on the network devices. These settings typically include parameters such as the BGP Autonomous System (AS) number, neighbor IP addresses, route policies, and prefix filters. In a large network, these configurations may vary depending on the location, device role, or connection type, and manually configuring each device can be a time-consuming and error-prone task. With Ansible, these configurations can be defined in a single playbook that is easily reusable and adaptable to different devices or environments.

Ansible provides specific modules for interacting with network devices and configuring routing protocols like BGP. For example, the ios_bgp module for Cisco devices can be used to configure BGP settings such as AS number, neighbor relationships, and route redistribution.

Similarly, the junos_bgp module can be used for Juniper devices, allowing administrators to automate the configuration of BGP settings across a range of devices with a consistent set of tasks. By using these modules, network administrators can ensure that BGP configurations are applied uniformly across all devices, reducing the risk of inconsistencies and errors.

One of the key advantages of using Ansible for automating BGP configurations is its ability to simplify the management of multiple devices. In large networks, BGP configurations may need to be applied to dozens or even hundreds of routers and switches. Doing this manually would require accessing each device individually, which is both time-consuming and inefficient. With Ansible, a single playbook can be written to configure BGP on multiple devices simultaneously. Ansible uses an inventory file to define the devices on which the playbook will be executed, and it can run tasks in parallel across all devices, ensuring that changes are applied consistently and quickly. This parallel execution significantly reduces the time required to implement BGP configurations across large networks.

Ansible also allows for the dynamic customization of BGP configurations based on variables. This is especially useful in environments where different devices have different BGP settings. For example, a router in one location may have a different AS number or neighbor configuration than a router in another location, but both devices need to run similar BGP configurations. By defining these settings as variables in the Ansible playbook or inventory file, administrators can ensure that the correct configuration is applied to each device. Ansible will substitute the variables with the appropriate values during execution, ensuring that each device receives the correct configuration without the need for manual updates. This level of customization allows for greater flexibility in managing BGP configurations across diverse network environments.

Another benefit of using Ansible for BGP configuration is the ability to automate the verification and validation of BGP settings. Once the BGP configuration has been applied, administrators need to ensure that the BGP session is established correctly and that routes are being advertised and received as expected. Ansible allows for the automation of this verification process, making it possible to check BGP status, neighbor relationships, and route advertisements across all devices in the network. For example, Ansible can be used to run commands like show ip bgp summary or show bgp neighbor on Cisco devices to retrieve information about the BGP session and ensure that it is functioning correctly. This automation not only saves time but also ensures that BGP configurations are verified consistently across the network.

Ansible also supports the use of templates, which can be particularly useful for generating dynamic BGP configuration files. For example, an administrator may need to generate a BGP configuration that includes specific network prefixes or policies for each device. By using Jinja2 templates, administrators can create configuration files that automatically incorporate these variables. The template can be populated with device-specific information, such as the local AS number, neighbor IP addresses, or route maps, and Ansible will dynamically generate the appropriate configuration for each device. This ensures that the configuration is both accurate and consistent, reducing the risk of manual errors and ensuring that the BGP configuration is aligned with the network's requirements.

One of the challenges in large networks is managing BGP route policies and filters. BGP policies, such as prefix lists, route maps, and filtering rules, play a critical role in controlling the flow of routing information. Automating the configuration of these policies can help ensure that they are consistently applied across all devices and reduce the risk of configuration drift. Ansible can be used to automate the creation and management of BGP route policies by defining them in the playbook and applying them to the appropriate devices. Whether it's setting up prefix filtering or configuring inbound or outbound route maps, Ansible allows administrators to automate these processes and ensure that BGP policies are enforced uniformly.

In large-scale networks, BGP configurations are constantly changing, whether due to network expansions, new peerings, or policy changes. Ansible's automation capabilities allow for rapid adjustments to be made when these changes occur. Rather than manually updating each device's BGP configuration, administrators can modify the Ansible playbook and quickly apply the changes across all relevant devices. This ensures that BGP configurations are always up to date and consistent with the network's evolving requirements. Additionally, the use of version control systems like Git with Ansible enables administrators to track changes to BGP configurations over time, providing a clear audit trail and making it easier to roll back changes if needed.

Ansible's ability to automate BGP configuration brings significant advantages in terms of efficiency, consistency, and scalability. By using Ansible, network administrators can quickly and reliably configure BGP across multiple devices, ensuring that settings are applied correctly and consistently. Ansible also simplifies the verification and validation of BGP configurations, automates the management of BGP policies, and supports dynamic generation of configuration files through templates. In large and complex networks, Ansible provides a powerful tool for managing BGP, reducing the manual effort required and improving network reliability. As BGP becomes an even more critical part of network infrastructure, automating its configuration with Ansible is an essential practice for maintaining a scalable and efficient network.

Cloud Networking Automation with Ansible and NETCONF

As cloud computing continues to grow and dominate the IT landscape, the need for efficient and scalable network management in cloud environments becomes increasingly important. Cloud networks are complex, dynamic, and often involve multiple virtualized and physical resources, making traditional network management techniques cumbersome and prone to errors. In this context, automation plays a pivotal role in ensuring that cloud networking environments are configured, monitored, and maintained efficiently. Ansible and NETCONF, two powerful tools in the network automation space, can be leveraged together to simplify the configuration and management of cloud network devices, providing a scalable, consistent, and flexible solution for network administrators.

Ansible is an open-source automation platform widely used for configuration management, application deployment, and task automation. It is known for its simplicity and ease of use, using YAML-based playbooks to define tasks that can be executed across multiple devices. NETCONF (Network Configuration Protocol) is a network management protocol that enables standardized configuration, monitoring, and retrieval of device data in XML format. NETCONF works with YANG data models to provide a structured approach to network management, making it ideal for automating cloud networking tasks. By combining Ansible and NETCONF, network administrators can create automated workflows that simplify the configuration of cloud network infrastructure, reduce manual intervention, and ensure consistency across a distributed cloud environment.

One of the primary benefits of using Ansible in cloud networking automation is its ability to manage a wide range of devices and cloud network components, from physical routers and switches to virtualized network functions and cloud-based services. With Ansible, network administrators can automate the deployment of network configurations across diverse cloud platforms, including public, private, and hybrid cloud environments. This can include configuring network interfaces, setting up virtual networks, and applying network policies to ensure that data flows securely and efficiently across the cloud infrastructure. By defining cloud network configurations in Ansible playbooks, administrators can ensure that the same set of configurations is applied uniformly to all cloud resources, regardless of their location or provider.

NETCONF complements Ansible by providing a structured and standardized way to configure and manage network devices. NETCONF supports a variety of device types, from legacy hardware to modern virtualized appliances, and enables network engineers to automate device configurations through a consistent interface. NETCONF's use of YANG data models ensures that network configurations are both machine-readable and consistent across different network devices. In a cloud networking environment, NETCONF can be used to automate the configuration of network devices, such as routers, switches, firewalls, and load balancers, ensuring that they are aligned with the overall cloud network architecture.

When combined, Ansible and NETCONF can provide a powerful solution for automating the configuration of cloud networking components. For instance, administrators can write Ansible playbooks that use NETCONF to configure network devices in a cloud environment. These playbooks can include tasks for configuring BGP (Border Gateway Protocol), applying VLAN configurations, or setting up routing protocols across cloud network devices. NETCONF can retrieve real-time operational data from these devices, allowing administrators to automate monitoring tasks and ensure that the cloud network is performing optimally. For example, NETCONF can be used to check interface statuses, gather performance statistics, or verify the state of network services across the cloud infrastructure, while Ansible can automate actions based on this data, such as applying configuration changes or sending alerts.

In cloud networking, scalability is critical. The dynamic nature of cloud environments means that devices and network components may frequently change, requiring network configurations to be adjusted accordingly. Ansible and NETCONF work together to automate these adjustments, ensuring that cloud networks can scale quickly and efficiently without compromising consistency or performance. For instance, as new instances are launched in a cloud environment, Ansible can automatically configure the necessary networking components, such as assigning IP addresses, configuring subnets, and applying security policies. NETCONF ensures that the configuration is applied in a structured and standardized way, ensuring that new network components integrate seamlessly into the existing infrastructure.

One of the key challenges in cloud networking is maintaining consistency across distributed environments. As cloud networks grow, managing configurations across multiple cloud regions, data centers, and virtualized components becomes increasingly difficult. Manual configuration processes are not only time-consuming but can lead to inconsistencies and errors that affect network performance and security. By automating network configuration with Ansible and NETCONF, administrators can ensure that cloud network settings are consistently applied, regardless of the scale or complexity of the environment. With Ansible, administrators can define reusable playbooks that apply cloud network configurations across multiple devices and locations, ensuring that the same settings are applied uniformly across the entire infrastructure.

NETCONF also plays an important role in maintaining the integrity of cloud networks by providing real-time monitoring and verification of network configurations. In a cloud environment, where resources are continuously deployed, modified, and decommissioned, it is crucial to verify that the network configurations are applied as intended. NETCONF enables administrators to retrieve real-time data from network devices, such as interface statuses, routing tables, and traffic statistics. This data can be used to monitor the health and performance of the cloud network and ensure that the configurations remain consistent over time. With NETCONF, administrators can automate checks and validation tasks to verify that the network is operating according to the desired state, reducing the likelihood of misconfigurations or performance issues.

Security is another crucial aspect of cloud networking, and automating security configurations is essential for maintaining a secure cloud infrastructure. Ansible and NETCONF can be used to automate the application of security policies across the cloud network, including firewall rules, access control lists (ACLs), and encryption settings. For example, administrators can use Ansible to define security policies in playbooks and apply them across cloud devices through NETCONF. NETCONF ensures that these policies are applied consistently, while Ansible automates the process of managing and updating security configurations as the cloud network evolves. This approach reduces the risk of human error, ensures that security policies are always up to date, and improves the overall security posture of the cloud infrastructure.

As cloud networking environments become more complex, the need for efficient and automated management solutions continues to grow. By leveraging Ansible and NETCONF, network administrators can streamline the process of configuring, managing, and monitoring cloud network devices, ensuring that the cloud infrastructure remains scalable, consistent, and secure. The combination of Ansible's flexibility and NETCONF's structured approach to configuration management enables administrators to automate the entire lifecycle of cloud networking, from initial configuration to ongoing maintenance and monitoring. This results in a more agile, reliable, and secure cloud network that can support the demands of modern businesses and applications.

The ability to automate cloud network configurations with Ansible and NETCONF allows organizations to manage their cloud resources more efficiently and with greater precision. By removing the need for manual intervention, automating network configurations reduces the risk of errors, accelerates deployment times, and enhances the overall performance of the network. With the growing complexity of cloud networking, automating network management tasks is no longer a luxury but a necessity for organizations looking to remain competitive and ensure the reliability of their cloud infrastructure.

Automating Data Center Networking with Ansible

Data centers are the backbone of modern IT infrastructure, providing the necessary resources for organizations to run applications, store data, and support digital services. With the increasing demand for higher availability, performance, and scalability, data center networking has become increasingly complex. As networks grow and evolve, managing the configuration and operation of network devices manually becomes cumbersome and prone to errors. Ansible, an open-source automation tool, provides an efficient and scalable solution for automating data center networking tasks. By using Ansible to automate tasks such as network configuration, monitoring, and management, data center administrators can improve efficiency, reduce human error, and ensure that the network remains reliable and secure.

Ansible is widely known for its simplicity and power in automating IT tasks, using YAML-based playbooks to define and execute tasks on network devices and servers. Ansible's agentless architecture means it can interact with a wide variety of network devices, including switches, routers, firewalls, and load balancers, by using standard protocols like SSH or NETCONF. This flexibility makes Ansible an ideal tool for automating data center networking. Network administrators can write playbooks to automate tasks such as configuring VLANs, managing IP addresses, adjusting routing protocols, or implementing security policies across hundreds or thousands of devices in the data center.

One of the most significant benefits of automating data center networking with Ansible is the ability to streamline network configuration. In large data centers, network devices must be consistently configured to ensure smooth communication between various servers, storage systems, and other network devices. Manually configuring each device can be time-consuming, error-prone, and difficult to scale. Ansible allows administrators to define network configurations in playbooks, which can then be automatically applied to all relevant devices. For example, a playbook can be written to configure VLANs across multiple switches, ensuring that all devices in a particular VLAN are correctly connected and can communicate with each other. This automated approach not only saves time but also ensures that the configurations are applied consistently across the data center, reducing the risk of misconfigurations that could lead to network outages or performance degradation.

In addition to basic configuration tasks, Ansible can be used to automate more complex network management functions, such as routing protocol configuration and traffic optimization. Data centers often rely on dynamic routing protocols like OSPF (Open Shortest Path First) or BGP (Border Gateway Protocol) to route traffic efficiently across the network. Configuring these protocols manually on each device can be cumbersome, especially in large-scale environments. By using Ansible, network administrators can automate the configuration of these protocols across multiple devices, ensuring that routing policies are consistently applied and updated across the entire data center. Ansible can also automate the configuration of quality of service (QoS) policies, which prioritize certain types of network traffic to ensure optimal performance for mission-critical applications. With Ansible, administrators can define QoS policies in playbooks, and these policies can be automatically applied to all network devices that require them, reducing the time and effort involved in configuring these settings manually.

Another critical aspect of data center networking is security, and automation plays a crucial role in ensuring that security policies are consistently applied across the network. In a data center, security policies must be enforced at multiple layers of the network, from the perimeter firewalls to internal access control lists (ACLs) and virtual private networks (VPNs). Managing these security policies manually is not only time-consuming but also increases the risk of errors that could leave the network vulnerable to attacks. Ansible allows administrators to automate the application of security policies, ensuring that they are uniformly enforced across all network devices. For example, Ansible can be used to automate the configuration of firewalls, applying consistent security rules across multiple devices to prevent unauthorized access. Similarly, Ansible can automate the setup of VPNs, enabling secure communication between different parts of the data center or remote locations.

Ansible's ability to automate the management and configuration of virtualized network devices is particularly beneficial in modern data centers, where virtualization plays a key role in resource efficiency and scalability. In virtualized environments, network devices may be virtualized themselves, running on hypervisors alongside virtual machines (VMs) and containers. Managing the network configurations of virtual devices can be more complex than managing physical devices, as the virtual devices may be provisioned and decommissioned dynamically. Ansible provides a flexible platform for automating the configuration and management of virtualized network devices, ensuring that network settings are correctly applied even as the virtual infrastructure evolves. Whether it's configuring virtual switches, managing virtual firewalls, or applying network policies to virtualized environments, Ansible can automate these tasks, helping administrators maintain a consistent and efficient network in a dynamic virtual environment.

Automation also plays a critical role in data center network monitoring and troubleshooting. While Ansible is primarily used for configuration management, it can also be used to automate network monitoring tasks, helping administrators ensure that the network is operating as expected. Ansible can automate the collection of performance metrics from network devices, such as interface statistics, link utilization, and error rates. This data can then be analyzed to identify potential issues before they escalate into problems. For instance, if a particular switch is experiencing high traffic or packet loss, Ansible can automatically trigger actions such as adjusting traffic routing, reconfiguring QoS policies, or alerting network administrators. By automating these monitoring tasks, Ansible enables administrators to maintain a high level of visibility into the network's health and performance, reducing the time required to detect and resolve issues.

In large-scale data center environments, maintaining consistency and preventing configuration drift is a significant challenge. Configuration drift occurs when devices become misconfigured over time due to manual changes, updates, or inconsistencies in the configuration process. This can lead to network outages, security vulnerabilities, and performance degradation. With Ansible, network configurations are stored as code in playbooks, making it easy to apply consistent configurations across all devices. By versioning the playbooks and maintaining them in a version control system, administrators can ensure that the configurations are always aligned with the intended state. If discrepancies are detected, Ansible can be used to automatically bring the devices back into compliance, preventing configuration drift and ensuring that the network remains stable and secure.

As data centers continue to grow and evolve, the need for scalable and flexible automation solutions becomes even more critical. Ansible provides an ideal platform for managing the complexity of modern data center networks. By automating tasks such as network configuration, security policy enforcement, and monitoring, Ansible reduces the manual effort required to manage large-scale networks, improves consistency across devices, and ensures that the network is always performing at its best. The ability to automate network management not only saves time but also enables network administrators to focus on higher-level tasks, such as designing new network architectures, optimizing performance, and ensuring security.

The integration of Ansible into data center networking workflows enables administrators to build agile, responsive, and efficient networks that can support the dynamic needs of modern businesses. By automating routine tasks and simplifying the management of complex networks, Ansible enhances the ability of data centers to scale quickly and meet the demands of growing organizations. Whether managing physical or virtual network devices, enforcing security policies, or monitoring network health, Ansible provides a powerful toolset for managing the intricacies of data center networking. Through automation, Ansible helps administrators maintain a high level of control over the network, ensuring that it operates smoothly, securely, and efficiently.

Future Trends in Network Automation and Ansible

As networks become increasingly complex and integral to business operations, the demand for network automation continues to rise. Network automation, the process of using software and tools to automatically configure, manage, and monitor network devices, has already transformed the way networks are operated. As we look to the future, the evolution of network automation technologies, particularly in conjunction with tools like Ansible, promises to further revolutionize how networks are managed. The future of network automation will be shaped by the growing need for agility, efficiency, and scalability in increasingly dynamic environments. Ansible, an open-source automation platform, is at the forefront of this transformation, providing a flexible, scalable, and extensible solution to meet the challenges of modern network management.

One of the most significant trends in network automation is the increasing adoption of software-defined networking (SDN) and network function virtualization (NFV). These technologies decouple network control and data planes, allowing for more agile and flexible network configurations. With SDN, network administrators can control the flow of data across the network programmatically using centralized controllers. NFV enables the virtualization of network functions, such as firewalls, load balancers, and routers, which are traditionally handled by dedicated hardware. As SDN and NFV continue to grow, Ansible's role in automating these environments will expand. Ansible's modular architecture allows it to integrate seamlessly with SDN controllers and NFV platforms, enabling administrators to automate network configurations and management tasks across both physical and virtualized network components. The ability to manage SDN and NFV deployments with Ansible will make networks more dynamic and flexible, enabling faster provisioning, scaling, and changes in response to evolving business needs.

Another trend driving the future of network automation is the growing importance of cloud-native architectures. Cloud computing has already had a profound impact on how networks are designed, deployed, and managed. As organizations increasingly adopt cloud-native principles, networks must become more integrated with cloud platforms and services. The rise of multi-cloud and hybrid-cloud environments, where organizations use a combination of public and private cloud infrastructure, presents a unique challenge for network management. Automating network configurations across multiple cloud environments is becoming a critical need for many organizations. Ansible's cloud integration capabilities make it a powerful tool for automating network configurations in cloud-native environments. Ansible can interact with cloud providers like AWS, Azure, and Google Cloud to automate network resource provisioning, security configurations, and network monitoring. As cloud-native environments continue to grow, Ansible will play an essential role in bridging the gap between traditional on-premise networks and cloud infrastructure.

The increasing complexity of networks, coupled with the rising volume of devices and traffic, will also drive the future of network automation toward more intelligent and self-healing systems. Machine learning and artificial intelligence (AI) are poised to revolutionize the way networks are managed and optimized. As networks become more data-driven, automation tools like Ansible will incorporate more AI and machine learning capabilities to automate not only the configuration of network devices but also their optimization and troubleshooting. AI can be used to predict network failures, detect anomalies, and suggest optimizations based on historical performance data. Ansible can then automate the implementation of these optimizations, making networks more adaptive and resilient. For example, an AI-driven system could detect congestion in a specific part of the network and automatically adjust routing protocols or QoS settings using Ansible, preventing performance degradation and ensuring a seamless experience for end users. The integration of AI and Ansible will create a more proactive network management paradigm, where systems can predict and resolve issues before they affect performance or availability.

Security will also continue to be a major focus in the future of network automation. As networks become more complex and interconnected, security threats become increasingly sophisticated. Automating security configurations and monitoring will be critical to maintaining secure networks at scale. Ansible has already demonstrated its ability to automate security policies across network devices, but as threats evolve, the demand for automated, dynamic security configurations will grow. Automation will be essential for managing network security in real-time, from configuring firewalls and VPNs to applying intrusion prevention systems (IPS) and network segmentation. As cybersecurity tools become more integrated with network management systems, Ansible will continue to evolve to automate the application of security measures in response to real-time threats. For example, Ansible could be used to automatically reconfigure network firewalls in response to detected threats or to adjust access control policies when a breach is suspected. The ability to automate security response and threat mitigation will help organizations stay ahead of potential vulnerabilities and ensure the integrity of their networks.

The concept of intent-based networking (IBN) is also gaining momentum as a future trend in network automation. IBN is an approach where network administrators define high-level business or operational goals, and the network automatically configures itself to meet those goals. For example, an administrator might specify that a certain application needs to be prioritized to ensure low latency, and the network would automatically adjust routing, QoS, and bandwidth settings to meet that objective. Ansible's flexibility makes it well-suited for supporting IBN workflows by automating the configuration of network devices in response to high-level intentions. As IBN becomes more prevalent, Ansible will play an integral role in transforming high-level business objectives into specific network configurations, reducing the time and effort required to implement complex network changes.

Another important aspect of future network automation is the continued shift towards infrastructure as code (IaC). IaC is the practice of managing and provisioning network infrastructure through code, rather than through manual configuration or physical hardware changes. This trend is closely related to the DevOps movement, where software development and IT operations are integrated to deliver continuous delivery of applications and services. By using IaC, network administrators can define network configurations and policies in code, making it easier to manage and automate network resources. Ansible has already established itself as a powerful tool for implementing IaC in network automation, allowing network configurations to be defined as code in playbooks and version-controlled in repositories. As IaC continues to grow in importance, Ansible's ability to manage and deploy network infrastructure as code will become even more vital, enabling teams to automate network provisioning, configuration, and updates in a seamless and efficient manner.

The future of network automation with Ansible will also involve deeper integration with other IT systems and workflows. As networks become more integrated with other parts of the IT ecosystem, such as application development, security, and cloud infrastructure, there will be a greater need for cross-platform automation. Ansible's extensibility and ability to integrate with a wide range of technologies make it an ideal platform for orchestrating end-to-end automation across the entire IT infrastructure. This will enable network administrators to automate not only network configurations but also network security, performance monitoring, and service provisioning, ensuring that all components of the IT environment work together seamlessly.

As networks become more sophisticated and the demand for automation continues to increase, the role of tools like Ansible in network management will only become more critical. From managing complex cloud environments and integrating AI-driven automation to enhancing security and supporting intent-based networking, Ansible is poised to be a cornerstone of the future of network automation. With its flexibility, scalability, and growing ecosystem, Ansible will continue to provide network administrators with the tools they need to efficiently manage and automate their networks, ensuring that they can meet the demands of an increasingly digital and interconnected world.